MW00795858

Praise for *The Brand Benefits Playbook*

"Allen and Debbie's book on positioning and brand benefits is a must-read for anyone seeking expert insights in this field. Their exceptional qualifications as thought leaders and innovators, backed by successful projects resulting in billions in shareholder value, make them unparalleled in advancing the science and art of positioning and brand promise. Through their accessible and actionable approach, they offer a unique blend of original research, academic work, and hands-on experience, making the journey into strategy both enlightening and enjoyable."

—**Jeff Hudson**, CEO, Venafi

"There's an old adage that marketing is about selling the sizzle and not the steak. It would be more accurate to say that it is about selling benefits, and *The Brand Benefits Playbook* provides readers with a master class. In a world where consumers are besieged by an onslaught of parity products, services, and brands, there's never been a better time for marketers to step back and consider how the benefits perceived by consumers can lead to better segmentation, targeting, and positioning strategies."

—**Larry Vincent**, former Chief Branding Officer, United Talent Agency (UTA)

"Allen and Debbie have built a profound yet simple model and process that identifies and aligns your brand benefits and segmentation to optimize and activate those benefits in your go-to-market positioning. They have not only been teaching these core concepts in positioning and branding for many years at the university level but also leveraging that unmatched knowledge to help position and build some of the largest and well-known brands in the world."

—**Joe Terry**, CEO, Culture Partners

"This book is a treasure trove of valuable advice for leaders focused on developing and leveraging their brands for growth. It offers play-by-play advice that moves strategy from the customer back into the organization's decisions, competencies, and culture to find a powerful and defensible way to go to and win in any market. If you want growth, you should read this book."

—**Christine Moorman**, T. Austin Finch, Sr. Professor of Business Administration, Duke University's Fuqua School of Business, and Founder and Director, The CMO Survey

"Debbie and Allen are *the* preeminent experts on branding and positioning, two often-misunderstood pillars of modern marketing. They speak in practical, accessible terms yet always with a critical, broader view that puts their ideas into a larger, deeper context."

—**Ann Handley**, bestselling Author, *Everybody Writes*, and Keynote Business Speaker

the **BRAND BENEFITS PLAYBOOK**

the BRAND BENEFITS PLAYBOOK

Why Customers Aren't Buying What You're Selling—And What to Do About It

Allen Weiss and Deborah J. MacInnis

Matt Holt Books
An Imprint of BenBella Books, Inc.
Dallas, TX

Matt Holt is an imprint of BenBella Books, Inc.
10440 N. Central Expressway
Suite 800
Dallas, TX 75231
benbellabooks.com
Send feedback to feedback@benbellabooks.com

Printed in the United States of America
10 9 8 7 6 5 4 3 2 1

Library of Congress Control Number: 2023031802
ISBN 9781637745038 (hardcover)
ISBN 9781637745045 (electronic)

Editing by Katie Dickman
Copyediting by Leah Baxter
Proofreading by Doug Johnson and Becky Maines
Text design and composition by PerfecType, Nashville, TN
Author photos by Bradford Rogne Photography
Cover design by Brigid Pearson
Printed by Lake Book Manufacturing

To Ryan, Katie, Stacy, and Tommy

CONTENTS

INTRODUCTION

Some of the greatest thinkers in business have emphasized the power of a customer-focused perspective; namely, focusing on what customers want from the things they buy and use. *The Brand Benefits Playbook* expands on this perspective, showing that a focus on the benefits that customers want in the brands they buy can provide an integrated lens on marketing decision-making—from market segmentation, to target segment selection, to brand positioning, and more.

Indeed, the various "plays" in the playbook provide a systematic, step-by-step approach to the marketing of new brands and existing ones. This integrated perspective is important and unique since marketing decision-making typically lacks a coherent framework. The plays in our playbook are applicable to any marketed entity; not just products or services but also large organizations, small businesses, start-ups, experiences, people, nonprofits, and even musical bands! They are also relevant to marketers in business-to-business (B2B) and business-to-consumer (B2C) markets.

Additionally, most marketing problems can be addressed when organizations focus on the benefits that customers want. For example, consider some examples of problems our clients have commonly expressed:

- Competitive Pressures
  - "We're losing too much business to our competitors."
  - "We seem to be in a commodity market."
- Messaging Problems
  - "Our messaging doesn't resonate like it used to."
  - "Our messaging is all over the place . . . we need to get clear."
- New Product Launches
  - "We have launched a new product and don't know why sales are so slow."
  - "We're not sure how to easily explain our product's features to customers."
- Top-of-the-Funnel Problems
  - "We're not targeting the right customers."
  - "Our salespeople are going after the wrong customers."

The playbook that we propose shows how all these problems (and more) can be addressed through the lens of brand benefits. Before we dive in, let's look at each "play" in the playbook.

- Play #1 introduces the concept of benefits. We describe the types of benefits that customers might want in whatever they buy and use and show how a focus on benefits can help all kinds of organizations: from mom-and-pop shops to Fortune 100 organizations. We describe why this focus on benefits works and articulate practical ways to identify what benefits customers in your market want.

- Play #2 emphasizes your brand and how customers perceive it now in terms of its benefits. We show why we emphasize brands rather than products. We also introduce the concept of perceptual maps, which provide insight into how customers perceive your brand now and how your brand's positioning might change.
- Play #3 allows you to view the brand benefits that operate in your market and how you can segment your market on these benefits.
- Play #4 describes how to choose a target segment based on your market segmentation results and articulate how your brand should be positioned to this target segment in terms of the benefits that are most important to them.
- Play #5 examines whether the positioning you propose for your brand is credible given the strengths of your organization.
- Play #6 articulates whether the positioning you propose is defensible given the competitive marketplace in which you operate.
- Play #7 presents a replay of a case study that uses a real-world example to illustrate the foundational ideas associated with Plays #1 through 6.
- Play #8 shows how to make your positioning resonate with customers throughout the customer journey (from prepurchase, to usage, to postpurchase judgments).
- Play #9 describes strategies for growing your brand based on its benefits. For example, Nike started out as a running shoe company, but the brand's focus on the benefit of "sports performance" has allowed it expand to myriad products for which sports performance is essential, including other sports shoes, sportswear, sports gear, and more.

Throughout the book we illustrate these ideas using real-world examples and insights from our own research and consulting experiences.

Our Road to This Book

So, how did we become interested in the ideas in this book? Here is a brief background.

Allen first learned about positioning a product as a newly minted assistant professor in the Graduate School of Business at Stanford University. Though he'd just received his PhD in marketing from the University of Wisconsin, he was an unlikely pick for Stanford, given his earlier career as a professional musician. Although his band never scored a record deal, they played throughout the country, often as the opening act for major recording stars like Lynyrd Skynyrd, Bonnie Raitt, and Kenny Loggins. While you might not think this has anything to do with brand benefits, it does—keep reading!

At the University of Wisconsin, Allen's PhD dissertation in marketing was good enough to land him a job at a major university. But before that happened, some highly ranked schools thought his background was, well, just too strange. During an interview at Harvard, the faculty openly wondered if he was a dilettante (Allen's vita listed his degrees in engineering, counseling psych, management, and marketing) and questioned his ability to handle their demanding MBA students. Allen told them he was able to manage, with confidence, a cherry bomb thrown onstage during a show at a bar in Missoula, Montana. So yes, he would be able to handle demanding MBA students.

In contrast, the marketing faculty at Stanford thought Allen's experience performing in front of crowds was an asset. The Introduction to Marketing class he would be teaching involved learning and teaching the formal aspects of positioning a product. As the faculty noticed, every musician implicitly knows about positioning, because they understand what connects with their audience and can deliver on it. He was able to connect what he would be teaching with his real-world experience, giving students a valuable and unique view of positioning. Eventually, he would teach positioning in the Executive Program at Stanford as well as other programs worldwide.

As a teacher, Allen quickly learned that positioning was aimed at a segment of the market and not the whole market. Segments were simply groups of customers who cared about the same things when considering a product or service. But what were these things customers cared about?

About this time, Allen came across a well-known quote by Harvard's Ted Levitt: "People don't want to buy a quarter-inch drill. They want a quarter-inch hole." The idea is that customers care less about what features a product has than about the benefits it provides. This seemed reasonable given Allen's experiences in music: audiences like the music, sure, but what they like even more are the emotional and social experiences they derive from listening to it. So, he reasoned that if you focus on benefits when positioning a brand, you are focusing on what customers really want. In addition, he learned that to track a brand's (and its competitors') current and future positioning requires a *perceptual map*. A perceptual map captures how customers in the market perceive your brand relative to competitors' brands based on the benefits that customers want. Over time, it became clear that a benefit focus helps you see potential competitors more clearly, and it helps the organization develop new product ideas.

Allen began teaching MBA students about segmentation, perceptual maps, and positioning using Levitt's idea of benefits as well as the concept of marketing myopia, a potentially deadly outcome that has befallen organizations and industries that focus on what their organization or product provides as opposed to what customers want. When teaching in executive programs, Allen always asked participants how they positioned their products. He never once heard a response about the benefits that customers want.

A few years after joining the Stanford faculty, Allen invited Jeff Hudson to be a guest speaker in his class. Jeff had been the CEO of Visioneer, a company devoted to captured documents and photographs. At the time, Jeff was a senior vice president of corporate development at Informix Software, a relational database company. Once Jeff had seen Allen's work on positioning and benefits, he asked him to come to Informix to position one of their products. Informix was a company that mainly focused on the features of their database products, not its benefits. This is when Allen first formalized a systematic process for positioning products in an organization.

Over two days, Allen worked with about fifteen people to develop a shared belief framework about how Informix could best compete in the growing information systems market. Based on a shared understanding of the marketplace and customer benefits, their prime mission was to outline a clear and precise message to communicate Informix's role in the systems management market to customers.

What got the attention of the employees at Informix was Allen's segmentation of their market. Segmentation (dividing up the market into groups of customers who differ in the benefits they find important)—as well as a perceptual map (a visualization exercise that depicts how customers view the various products in the market in terms of their benefits)—gave them a new understanding of where they stood in the market and how the competition was entering and fortifying different segments. Someone called this view the "playing field" of marketing. At the end of the multiday workshop, after they'd constructed a unique positioning statement that resonated with everyone, the team applauded. They knew where they stood and how to move forward.

Over time, Allen became responsible for positioning most of the products at Informix, including their flagship database product. The company became a major player in relational databases for banks and other high-security industries and was eventually acquired by IBM.

Over the next few years, Allen moved to the University of Southern California and continued to work with numerous technology companies to help them position their products. In doing so, he continuously updated and refined his positioning process. He worked with satellite companies, music distributors, insurance agencies, banks, telecom companies, and more on their positioning and marketing strategies. After teaching an executive education class to Northrop Grumman and Hughes Space and Communications executives on competitive analysis, Allen's positioning process evolved to include a strong emphasis on competition and game theory. So, instead of simply identifying a position, Allen would ask clients to play out a competitive game. This exercise shows people how their competitors might respond to the organization's proposed positioning, what the organization might do in response to competitors' actions, and so on. By evaluating competitors' potential responses to the proposed positioning, his clients became convinced that the proposed positioning was highly defensible.

Positioning is a *promise* to the market, so it's up to organizations to *fulfill* that promise through their marketing activities. Like most consultants, Allen was not asked to stay around during the actual execution of his plans. The only way to know if the brands' success in the market could be attributed to the proposed positioning was to track whether the promise was fulfilled via a perceptual map.

With a great deal of experience teaching as well as positioning products and services for a wide variety of organizations, Allen teamed up with Debbie (coincidentally, his wife) and together we wrote this book. Debbie is a globally recognized multi-award-winning expert on evidence-based customer decision-making and brand strategies, emphasizing customer benefits. She has coauthored books and top journal articles on branding, including an award-winning research article on positioning and brand strategy. She is one of a handful of scholars who are fellows of the American Marketing Association, the Association for Consumer Research, and the Society for Consumer Psychology. Debbie was also named Distinguished Marketing Educator of 2023, an award given jointly by the American Marketing Association, Irwin, and McGraw Hill. She has also consulted with a broad range of organizations in such industries as life sciences, consumer packaged goods, advertising agencies, online ventures, and others. More relevant to this book, she has taught numerous customer-behavior courses; all with a focus on how understanding customers' desires and behaviors guides marketing decision-making. Debbie has also coauthored (with C. Whan Park and Andreas Eisingerich) a companion book to this one (titled *Brand Admiration: Building a Business People Love*) that emphasizes how a benefits-focused perspective can help organizations build brand admiration and sustain it over time. Combined, we bring eighty years of academic and real-world experiences to this book.

In our early discussions about the book, Allen would use the term *product*, and Debbie would call the same thing a *brand*. Allen's perspective was that of positioning a product—and he termed it product positioning. Eventually, Allen learned from Debbie that while organizations make products, customers buy brands. Debbie also introduced Allen to the various types of benefits that make up markets.

This book joins together the work Allen has done (mostly in the "business to business," or B2B, space) developing a rigorous process for positioning with Debbie's insights as an expert on benefits and brand strategy (mostly in the "business to consumer," or B2C, space). These two perspectives, when combined, provide a unique and integrated perspective on the playbook that marketers should follow when positioning a brand, executing on that positioning, and growing the brand. Indeed, the titles of our chapters outline the various "plays" that make up this playbook—the best way to operate within the "playing field" of marketing.

A final point before we begin: marketing, unlike most other functions in an organization, does not have a standard, agreed-on vocabulary. Because of the lack of standards, marketing language tends to be confusing. For this reason, and to make this text more accessible to any reader, we clearly identify key terms used in the book in **bold** and define them as they appear.

FOCUS ON BENEFITS

Let's start with the basics. To an organization, a **brand** (Tide) is a "value-generating entity," meaning that it earns revenue to organizations. To customers, a brand (Tide) is a name (often accompanied by a logo) that reflects what this entity gives them (its benefits) relative to other brands in the market.[1] **Benefits** are the desirable outcomes that customers expect to receive from your brand. This holds true whether those customers are in B2B or B2C spaces, and whether you sell a product, service, sporting event, entertainment product, nonprofit, cupcake, or anything else.[2] Benefits help customers reach their goals *and* reduce their pains.

Think about the benefits that consumer brands like Amazon provide and customers want. You get access to an incredible assortment of goods that provides the benefit of *finding what you need*. Reviews and questions regarding a particular product provide the benefit of *reassurance*—enhancing certainty that what you get is what you want. The ability to order items easily and know that they will come as soon as possible provides *convenience*. Amazon's benefits are entirely different than those of other retailers like Nordstrom. Yet Amazon faces competition from other retailers trying to offer the same benefits. To keep up, Amazon will need to either deliver higher levels of these benefits or add new ones.

Benefits are the desirable outcomes that customers receive from your brand.

Benefits can be inherent in the product itself: one of Häagen-Dazs's benefits includes its delightful taste. A high-performance computer processor provides the benefit of speed for whoever uses the computer. But benefits can also be realized through a transaction process. For example, an efficient transaction process (e.g., short checkout lines, ready access to customer service, secure ordering, and easy returns) provides the benefits of convenience and reduced frustration. Benefits can be realized when customers use and experience your brand, as when customers realize benefits like ease of use or pleasure from use. Some brands like Four Seasons, Taylor Swift, and the Pittsburgh Steelers have benefits that come when the brand is experienced (e.g., Four Seasons' luxurious accommodations, Taylor Swift's amazing songs, or the Steelers' exciting play). Customers can also realize benefits like a more organized home when they dispose of unneeded goods, as nonprofits like the Salvation Army and Goodwill realize.

Product features, attributes, or characteristics are important because they can give rise to the benefits that customers want.[3] But we should not confuse these product features with benefits. Features refer to what the product *has* or *offers*; benefits refer to what the product *does for customers* (see Exhibit 1.1). For example, a hand-tooled Birkin handbag costing $35,000 allows customers to signal their status to others (a benefit) so that customers feel pride and admiration from others (a goal). If you focus on features, you are missing what customers really want.

Features refer to what the product has or offers; benefits refer to what the product does for customers.

It's easy to confuse benefits with pain points or goals. You will often hear organizations focus on customers' pain, especially in B2B markets. The reduction of pain is a goal. Benefits are what the product provides so that customers can achieve their goals and eliminate their pains (again, see Exhibit 1.1). As you will learn in

EXHIBIT 1.1. How Benefits Relate to Brand Features and Customer Goals/Pain Relief

Product Features →	Benefits →	Goals/Pain That Benefits Solve
Three-ply facial mask	Protection from COVID	Staying healthy
24/7 store hours	Shopping convenience	Time flexibility
$35K hand-tooled handbag	Status-signaling potential	Feeling admired
Sustainably sourced ingredients	Supporting the planet	Living one's values
High-quality components	Reliability	Peace of mind

this book, if you focus on your customers' goals or pains, you will miss out on understanding what you need to do (what benefits to provide) to help customers reach their goals or relieve their pain.

If you're not convinced that customers want benefits, look around the room you're in right now and find something you own and like. Ask yourself, "Why did I buy that?" Sure, it might have some appealing features, but why did you want that feature? You liked it because it provided some benefits that you wanted.

Product reviews such as those in *Consumer Reports* typically evaluate and compare brands in terms of the benefits they provide to customers. Likewise, customers typically talk about the benefits they've experienced, such as speed, convenience, efficiency, comfort, and breathability, as opposed to specific product features.

TYPES OF BENEFITS

There are three types of benefits that customers might want from brands: functional, symbolic, and experiential.[4] You'll find examples of these types of benefits when you look at existing brands and markets.

Functional Benefits

Functional benefits provide solutions to problems and challenges so that customers feel that they have control over their environments.[5] Functional benefits also help customers by conserving limited resources, whether they be time and money or psychological and physical resources. Brands can enhance customers' limited resources through functional benefits—for example, by helping them earn money, sleep better, feel stronger, or be more knowledgeable.[6] Examples of functional benefits include reliability and durability (saving time and money, reducing stress, and providing a sense of control), convenience (saving time and making use easy), protection or safety (providing security and control), and information (providing knowledge and efficacy).

A recent client of ours in the training industry had customers looking for a wide variety of functional benefits, such as the ability to customize not only training but also the extent to which customers would get state-of-the-art training or how engaged users were in the training. Once we identified the benefits of their existing product, we helped the organization clearly see what types of customers they should be targeting. This was done by segmenting the market so they could understand which benefits each segment wanted and where the client had an advantage over their competitors. For example, one segment cared mostly about the breadth of available training topics and the observability of results, while another segment cared mostly about cost and the level of engagement of the training.

Many brands offer and promote functional benefits, as Exhibit 1.2 demonstrates. Functional benefits remove negative states and effectively help customers eliminate pain and achieve their goals. Think about the brands that your organization sells or that you, as a customer, buy. Chances are, you can identify brands that offer mostly functional benefits. These feelings contribute to happiness, as they make people feel capable, competent, empowered, secure, safe, relieved, assured, knowledgeable, and confident. Thus, functional benefits can be important motivators of brand purchases.

In many contexts, customers don't consider products in isolation. For example, you go to a shopping mall for clothes rather than a specific garment. You decide to upgrade your kitchen and bring in a designer, but to have your new kitchen become a reality requires electricians, plumbers, construction people, and much more. In a technology context, you might sell a digital signal processor, but the buyer needs a logic board as well.

In these situations, a functional benefit that customers want is convenience, or one-stop shopping. Some customers care deeply about one-stop shopping, which drives them to a department store, while others prefer boutique shops. Some customers want their kitchen designers to be "prime contractors" who handle all the plumbers, electricians, and other tradespeople involved in a kitchen remodel. To some customers in the database industry, a preference for one-stop shopping means that they want a database company (e.g., Oracle) whose software applications all work seamlessly together.

These examples illustrate the importance of understanding the customer's usage system. A usage system is where customers must use multiple products together to get value out of the group of products. Think of a smartphone and the service that it provides: talk, text, and data. A user can't get much use for smartphone if it offers only calls, or data, or text (they want all three). Understanding the customer's usage system is essential because customers' decisions can be based on the system, not just one part of the system. If customers need the whole system, then the benefits will be for that entire system, rather than one part (a particular product) within that system. If you don't sell the entire system, then your product must be compatible with the other parts of the usage system.

Experiential Benefits

Experiential benefits engage your customers' five senses (touch, sight, sound, smell, and taste), as well as their thoughts and feelings. If you've ever enjoyed—and we mean *really* enjoyed—a good meal at a restaurant or listened to good music, you know what we're talking about. A beautifully designed product or an aesthetically pleasing work of art both offer experiential benefits. So too do "person brands" like comedians, who arouse a customer's sense of humor. Experiential benefits have mood-regulating qualities, such that we are in a better mood once we experience them. For example, think about the experiential benefits you might receive after getting a massage. Chances are, you'd feel deeply relaxed afterward (at least, until you returned to the office!). Or imagine the most recent romantic comedy movie you watched, novel you read, or football game or concert you attended. Activities like these can make people feel warmhearted, entertained, engaged, and excited. These are experiential benefits too.

Lululemon advertises its experiential benefits with words like "soft, comfortable fabrics," "the feeling of a shoe made specifically for your foot? Pure bliss." Apple made the simple act of unboxing a new product into an experiential benefit by using a stunning box that made the phone seem like a gift. Eventually, unboxing became an internet fetish, and now all companies try to imitate what Apple started.

Nonprofits provide experiential (emotional) benefits when they show donors how their donations have helped those in need. Experiential benefits can make your customers feel gratified, entertained, stimulated, engaged, relaxed, nostalgic, or warmhearted. Think about your own organization and the brands you sell, as well as the brands you buy in your role as a customer. Consider which brands offer primarily experiential benefits.

Symbolic Benefits

The last type of benefit is symbolic. **Symbolic benefits** enrich customers by resonating with their identity: who they are, who they were, and who they want to be. Symbolic benefits thus "symbolize" desired aspects of one's identity. For example, brands can enhance someone's sense of belonging by making them feel part of a group with whom they do or wish to affiliate. Harley-Davidson enhanced this sense of belonging by creating a brand community of Harley-Davidson enthusiasts, the Harley Owners Group (HOG). Place-based brands (think the Green Bay Packers or the Chicago Cubs) can also enhance feelings of connectedness by highlighting customers' affiliations with where they live or the sports teams that they support. Some brands, like Gucci, Rolls-Royce, and Patek Philippe, are status brands that make customers feel special and privileged. Symbolic benefits also include feelings of doing the right thing, such as living in ways that are consistent with deeply held values. Patagonia offers symbolic benefits by appealing to consumers' desires to live sustainably and their values of universalism. Through symbolic benefits, your customers feel inspired, proud, unique, connected, or validated. Do any of the brands that your organization sells involve symbolic benefits? What are the symbolic benefits associated with the some of the brands you buy as a consumer?

Exhibit 1.2 provides examples of brands in different contexts and the possible benefits they might provide.

EXHIBIT 1.2. Possible Benefits for Different Categories (features in parentheses)

Category	Brand	Functional Benefits	Experiential Benefits	Symbolic Benefits
Products	Toyota Prius	Reliable; good value for the money; durable; safe (due to Toyota Safety Sense features); confidence in servicing (Toyota Genuine Parts)	Fun colors; smooth seats; stylish (due to aesthetically pleasing lines); good interior sound (via immersive multimedia system)	Earth friendly (due to hybrid motor)
Services	Hilton Hotels	Highly accessible (due to large number of hotels around the world); easy (online) reservations and check-in; safe (contactless arrival, Hilton CleanStay program, social distancing at conferences)	Comfortable (beds, pillow types, desk, robes, tub shower); tasty food (from upscale in-house restaurants); making memories (through wedding, conference, and family celebrations)	Exclusive benefits (from Hilton Honors membership); prestige (from becoming an elite member)

Category	Brand	Functional Benefits	Experiential Benefits	Symbolic Benefits
Ingredients	Morton Salt	Safety (from snow and ice melt properties); enabling plumbing durability (from water softening benefits); easy to buy (in major retailers and online)	Fun (from Morton salt water pool); tasty food (from seasonings)	Pride from usage (given Morton's commitment to racial and social justice)
Nonprofits	Girl Scouts of the USA	Building courage and confidence in young girls; accessible and convenient (troops across the US); opportunities to earn funding (through scholarships, grants, awards)	Fun (events and activities); good tasting (cookies)	Opportunities to give back (by being a volunteer, alum mentor, or through donations); connectedness to other girls and leaders; opportunities to showcase achievements (through badges)

Category	Brand	Functional Benefits	Experiential Benefits	Symbolic Benefits
Retailers	Trader Joe's	Good value for the money (competitive prices); convenient (parking, short lines at cashier); informative (recipes, guides, packages, customer updates)	Friendly (cashiers); delicious food products; interesting (changing product array)	Local belonging (each store reflects its neighborhood)
Media	CNN	Timely; credible; reliable information	A sense of immersion in the news (from vivid videos)	Sense of being an informed citizen

Organizations in B2B markets tend to focus on functional benefits, while customers in B2C markets tend to focus on brands with functional, symbolic, or experiential benefits. However, it is possible for B2B brands to offer experiential and symbolic benefits as well. Research has shown that the most admired brands have all three types of benefits.[7] For example, Nike offers the functional benefits of durable fabrics and safe, convenient, and accessible gear; the experiential benefits of soft, thermoregulating, and moisture-wicking fabric that feels good on the skin; and the symbolic benefits of inspiration, hope, and drive from challenging oneself to be a better athlete.

What this means is that brands can differentiate themselves and gain admiration if they get out of the trap of focusing only on functional benefits (or worse, focusing on their features). It also means that brands that offer one type of benefit (e.g., symbolic or experiential) might add value by offering other kinds of benefits. For example, Navistar truck manufacturing offers truckers the functional benefits of being safe, reliable, and convenient. Its spacious cab offers sufficient space for drivers to do whatever they need to do while on the road (work, sleep, relax, and eat). It also offers truckers experiential benefits. The cab (replete with hardwood floors and chrome) is comfortable and provides ample opportunities for entertainment (through a TV and seven-speaker Monsoon sound system). The company also offers symbolic benefits, making drivers feel that they are part of a brotherhood or community of drivers who drive Navistar's trucks.[8]

A brand can have more than one benefit and more than one type of benefit. For example, a brand could emphasize only functional benefits, like convenience, reliability, or affordability. Or it could offer multiple types of benefits, such as convenience, tastiness, and earth friendliness.

When thinking about brand benefits, it's important to consider whether brands provide certain benefits (yes or no), and how extensively the brand provides certain benefits (a little versus a lot). Brands can be differentiated when they *provide benefits that other brands do not.* They can also be differentiated by providing *greater levels of benefits* relative to competing brands. Benefits must also be evaluated in terms of their value or *importance* to customers. As we will see in chapter three, different customer segments can be identified based on how important various benefits are to those customers.

Brands can be differentiated when they provide benefits that other brands do not.

WHAT ABOUT PRICE?

In most markets, the price of a product or service is one element in customers' purchase decisions. Therefore, price should be included in any analysis of a market. But *by itself,* price is not a benefit. It is the cost customers pay to derive the benefits.

That said, in some markets—especially those with symbolic benefits—customers might regard a high price as a benefit because it signals exclusivity or prestige. In markets where exclusivity or prestige are not important, a high price would be regarded as a negative benefit (it would hurt purchase).

In other cases, customers evaluate price relative to their budgets. If the price is within (or outside) their budget, it will be regarded as affordable (or unaffordable). Affordability could be regarded as a positive benefit, while lack of affordability would be a negative benefit.

In still other cases, customers evaluate price relative to the benefits that they will receive from purchase versus the price and benefits of a competitor's product. A price that is seen as good given the benefits received is perceived as a "good value for the money." In such cases, judgments that the price is low given the benefits it provides could be regarded as a benefit.

So, while we include price in our analyses, it is not by itself a benefit. Keep this in mind as we move forward.

WHY BENEFITS MATTER

Marketing is not just a function. As the legendary management consultant Peter Drucker said, "[Marketing] is the whole business seen . . .

from the customer's point of view."[9] A *benefits focus emphasizes customers,* and as a result, your organization becomes more focused on your customer's perspective (see Exhibit 1.3 on page 35). Drucker also noted that profit is not the goal of business. It is a result that happens when organizations do a good job of delivering what customers want. Two central tenets of business include clarifying who the customers are and what they value.

A benefits approach is not in and of itself a new approach, but we have found that it is underutilized, leading organizations to leave money (and customers) on the table.

Beyond being customer-focused, an emphasis on customer benefits *makes your job easier*—and who doesn't want that? As we will discuss throughout this book, a benefits focus provides the lens for myriad marketing decisions. Remember, this holds true for any marketed entity, whether it's a product, store, service, nonprofit, or something else.

We show in this book that when your organization focuses on benefits, you're in a better position to understand:

- How to segment your market
- How customers currently perceive your brand in terms of its benefits
- Whether you should and can offer new benefits to attract more demand in a competitive marketplace
- How to select a target segment and determine the most viable way of positioning your brand in that market
- How to leverage what you need to know about delivering on those benefits throughout the customer journey
- How to grow your brand over time

Organizations have many important questions that span three levels: market, product, and organizational. Let's look at some of these questions and how a benefits focus can answer them, beginning with market-level reasons.

Market Reasons

This section discusses several market-level reasons for focusing on brand benefits. If your organization operates in a market where competition exists, it is natural to ask questions that deal with knowing the competition and identifying options for growth. If you focus on brand benefits, you will have a better understanding of how to address these questions. We show how in Exhibit 1.3 and in the following paragraphs.

Avoiding Marketing Myopia. One reason why benefits matter to companies and industries is that a benefit focus *avoids the problem of marketing myopia*. In 1960, Theodore Levitt discussed the classic example of how the invention of the automobile left the buggy-whip industry blindsided. Had people in the buggy-whip industry defined their market in terms of the benefits that customers wanted (i.e., efficient transportation), they might have anticipated the impact of the automobile and adjusted accordingly. Marketing myopia happens when we focus on a product, industry, vertical, or demographic instead of the benefits that customers want. Companies and industries can become blindsided by thinking too narrowly about their markets.

Consider the rise of rideshare services like Uber, as an alternative to taxicabs. The origin of the taxi can be traced back to the 1600s, when horse-drawn vehicles began being offered for hire. The modern taxi business was critical to many cities, like New York, as it provided transportation in and around urban areas. Under the medallion system, taxis operated with limited competition. While they competed with other modes of transport—buses, subways, private cars, shoe leather—there was often no other convenient way to get from one point to another in a city except by hailing or calling a taxi. When smartphones came out in the early 2000s, there was no attempt by the taxi industry to provide more control and certainty to consumers who used smartphones. Then, along came Uber in 2010 and Lyft in 2012. Taxi companies could not believe that anyone would jump in a car with an unlicensed stranger. But people valued the convenience benefits of hailing and paying for rides from their phones. Meanwhile, what had made taxis dominant—the centralized dispatch systems, limits on the supply of medallions, industry regulations, and more—suddenly became liabilities.

You move at your own peril if you think that marketing myopia won't affect your organization or industry. Organizations that regularly look to understand the benefits that their customers want and that are willing to reexamine their own business practices are less likely to get blindsided by market evolution. This is a clear advantage of adopting a brand benefits focus.

Seeing Potential Competitors. Taking a benefits perspective can also *help you see the full set of potential competitors,* and not get locked in on just the usual suspects. Competitors often enter a market by providing perceived higher performance on benefits than current providers. By focusing on customer benefits, you avoid being blindsided by new competitors and substitute products.

Allstate Insurance is in the highly competitive property and casualty insurance industry. One of the main benefits they provide is protecting your home and vehicles from disasters both small and large. An ad from Allstate Insurance showed their "Mayhem" character looking into a Ring doorbell, which the homeowner is viewing while away at a basketball game.[10] Mayhem tells the Ring doorbell owner that he will smash his car. "What? What?" says the ring doorbell owner as he watches his car being smashed and stolen. Allstate and Ring both offer the benefit of feeling safe at home, and the global doorbell camera market in particular has grown due to concerns of security, safety, and the well-being of individuals and families. Clearly, they are in different industries (insurance versus home security), so Allstate cannot compete directly with Ring by providing their own smart doorbell. But they can still position their products as competitive to Ring's. Focusing on customer benefits changes your perspective on where prospective competitors might come from.

With benefits as your starting point, it's a good practice to sit back and think not just about your immediate competitors, but also about other products that provide the same benefits. Keep your eyes open and think about competition broadly as you consider your market and the benefits that your customers seek.

For example, Coca-Cola says its purpose is to "refresh the world." By saying you are in the refreshment business (a benefits focus), rather than the soda business (a product focus), you open a broader view of the potential market and the competitors in that market.

Identifying Paths to Growth. As we'll discuss later in the book, a benefits approach also allows you to *identify new avenues for growth.* Consider Arm & Hammer. Originally sold as a baking soda product, the brand's deodorizing benefit allowed it to extend into all kinds of products for which deodorizing is important: kitty litter, car air fresheners, changing pads, air purifiers, diaper bags and pails, carpet cleaners, toothpaste, body wash, foot care, and more. Additionally, the deodorizing benefit has led to alliances with Dutch Boy paint and Hefty trash bags. In short, being a brand that is known for a particular benefit enables growth opportunities beyond the product's original focus.

Product Reasons

A benefit focus is also useful from the perspective of the products you do or could market.

Developing New Product Ideas. First, a benefit focus can also help you *develop new product ideas.* If you're a skeptical reader, you might wonder whether customers even know what benefits they want. In fact, maybe you've heard something like this from colleagues or friends: "I think assuming people know what they want and need in a product in the first place is a mistake because they simply don't, just like nobody knew that we needed an iPhone before the first iPhone was born." Indeed, when asked about consumer research on the iMac, Steve Jobs replied: "A lot of times, people don't know what they want until you show it to them."[11]

After all, nobody knew they wanted Alexa until Alexa was born, or Ring doorbells until they were launched, or PowerPoint until Microsoft came up with it. The list goes on, and people who make the list always have the same point: that customers don't know what they want until someone makes it first. Their argument also goes that people can't tell you anything about what they want until they see specific product features or attributes. Our argument is different.

At the time of the iPhone's launch in 2007, there were other phones and devices on the market, most notably the BlackBerry, launched in

1999. The device became so addictive—people were constantly checking their emails on it—that the device became known as a "CrackBerry."

How did the iPhone derive so much attention, and eventually take over the market from BlackBerry? Let's start by looking at the announcement of the iPhone: "Today, we're introducing three revolutionary products of this class," Jobs said. "The first one is a widescreen iPod with touch controls. The second is a revolutionary mobile phone. The third is a breakthrough Internet communications device . . . These are not three separate devices. This is one device. And we are calling it iPhone. Today, Apple is going to reinvent the phone."[12]

> ***Customers may not be able to tell you what*** **features or attributes** ***they want in a new product, but they can tell you what benefits they want.***

What were the iPhone's benefits when it first came out? Benefits like reliable phone service were significant, but these benefits were already available with the BlackBerry. But the convenience of having one product do the work of three products was new. While benefits like "I'm cool" or "I'm part of a group of tech-oriented people" were available with the BlackBerry, the iPhone pushed these benefits to a higher degree. That is, you might be cool with a BlackBerry, but it's cooler to own an iPhone (plus, you get other benefits like convenience). Even benefits like "It's something I can touch or something that feels great and makes my photos look great" were significantly better with the iPhone. Before long, the BlackBerry was completely overtaken by the iPhone.

Did the iPhone create benefits like being cool or having more convenience in your life? Was the benefit of convenience invented by

Apple? No. People already wanted these benefits. It's just that there were no products before the iPhone that delivered them—or delivered them to the degree that the iPhone did.

Apple was able to overpower the BlackBerry by continuing to focus on benefits that customers wanted and then adding features and attributes that supported those benefits. These benefits included providing a pleasing visual design (experiential benefits) in the product and stores, technology that was easy to use and learn (functional benefits), and a focus on status and coolness (symbolic benefits).

Another example of how a benefits focus drives product ideas comes from the work of Eric von Hippel from MIT. His research on "lead users" found that about 82 percent of all scientific instruments sold commercially and 63 percent of all semiconductor and electronic subassembly manufacturing equipment innovations he examined were developed *by customers*, not in-house by companies.[13] The implication is that when customers want benefits that no current product embodies, they will create their own product.

Von Hippel tells the story of customers using a glucose monitor, made by Dexcom, to measure blood sugar for type 1 diabetes and to see the results on the device.[14] The problem was that users had no way to track the data without the device being present. This was important to a father whose daughter used this device. The father couldn't let his daughter go on sleepovers for fear she would slip into a coma at night. The father found a community of other caregivers with the same need for the benefits of feeling safe and in control. They hacked the Dexcom device to send blood sugar data to the Internet so it could always be viewed remotely. In essence, they made a new product that provided the needed benefits (again, of feeling safe and in control). Whether or not you agree with the hacking, the point is that they were motivated and able to secure the benefits they needed.

Often, component suppliers develop products as well. Why does this happen? Because customers want benefits—and if no organization has come up with a product to satisfy those desired benefits, some customers create the products themselves.

The takeaway here is that if your organization can really tap into and understand the benefits that customers in your market are looking for, you can unlock enormous value by adopting a benefits-led approach to new product development (see Exhibit 1.3 on page 35).

Understanding Shocks and Trends. Another reason why benefits matter to organizations is that they can *help you understand the effects of shocks and trends.* Shocks are events that can affect what benefits customers want or how important existing benefits are to them. Shocks are like earthquakes. They send out tremors that rattle the status quo.

Let's think about the shocks to the system that occurred with the onset of the COVID pandemic. Suddenly, customers had desires for all kinds of new products that had the benefit of protecting their health. Demand for products such as face masks and amenities such as delivery services skyrocketed. As many of us spent more time at home, we placed greater importance on products both inside (furniture, TVs) and outside our homes (vegetable gardens, flowerpots). New platforms like Zoom added a benefit of interconnectivity, giving us a go-to way to perform our jobs at home or keep in touch with friends and family. Demand for puppies was unprecedented, as they gave some of us the benefit of connectedness to counteract the loneliness of social isolation. Given product shortages and supply chain problems, many of us placed greater importance on the benefit of product availability, even with mundane products like toilet paper.

The shocks to the system from COVID have made some benefits that were previously not important become more important. Companies like Amazon were well positioned for these shocks given the increased importance of the benefit of fast delivery. Other companies, like many restaurants, were caught off guard as the benefit of convenience (having meals delivered at home) and safety (having curbside and contactless pickup) became more important.[15] Some restaurants responded to these needed benefits and were able to survive.[16]

Likewise, economic, political, social, and cultural trends can affect the market offerings that customers want and the benefits they seek. Trends are like mountains that grow from pressure beneath the earth's surface. Consider the trend toward embracing multiculturalism. This trend increased the importance customers placed on identity-based products that showcased one's heritage. Multiculturalism also increased the importance customers placed on brands that support racial equality. This trend also affects how customers evaluate marketers that do or do not support cultural pluralism, and how they support brands that have earned a degree of cultural capital. Multiculturalism has also affected place-based brands such as New York and Los Angeles, which have diverse multiethnic neighborhoods that enhance the benefit of excitement of being part of these large cities.

Some shocks affect trends too. Take for example the murder of George Floyd. In response to that event's (literal) shock, many companies stepped up efforts to do more in their support of racial justice. For example, Apple, Meta, Pfizer, Johnson & Johnson, and Procter & Gamble made promises about what they would do, pledging to be a force for societal change. Consequently, customers wanted to see companies engage in genuine efforts to create such change (a symbolic benefit). Given the trend toward multiculturalism, these demands for companies to support racial justice took on added importance.

Because these environments constantly change, markets are dynamic. This dynamism can influence which benefits customers find important. For example, trends toward organic food and concerns about where foods are coming from have made consumers more willing to buy organic brands. These trends have helped those food companies that are transparent about where their foods are coming from.[17]

Organizational Reasons

A benefits focus is also useful from the perspective of your organization.

Helping Companies Financially. First, a benefit focus can *help companies financially* (see Exhibit 1.3).[18] In particular, when companies offer the functional, experiential, and symbolic benefits that customers want, customers are more likely to become loyal to the brand and advocate on its behalf. Such behaviors, in turn, reduce costs and build revenue. It costs less to offer a brand to which customers are already loyal. It also costs less to advertise when customers advertise on your brand's behalf through positive word of mouth (online or offline). If the brand they want is out of stock, they will defer purchase until the brand is in stock. Indeed, positive equity with customers is likely to affect a brand's financial performance.[19] As another example, one study examined the role of functional, symbolic, and experiential benefits on consumers' attachment or aversion to a large grocery chain operating in 33 countries around the world. The three types of benefits strongly predicted brand attachment, which in turn impacted total volume purchased, estimated future purchase, extent of purchase at the collaborating store vs. other grocery stores, and likelihood of participating in brand events.[20] The three types of benefits also influence consumers' commitment to the brand.[21]

Providing a Lens for Big Data and AI. The availability of massive amounts of customer-behavior data in some industries (e.g., consumer packaged goods) has promised to revolutionize how organizations conduct marketing. But real insights from such data often prove elusive. The reason why is because organizations have shifted their attention from customers to data acquisition and management. What is lost is an emphasis on customers and the benefits they seek. Big data and a benefits focus need not be mutually exclusive. Instead, benefits can *provide the lens through which organizations can develop insights from big data*. Researchers can examine patterns in data from the perspective of customer benefits.[22] A focus on benefits also helps us understand what data to collect in order to understand the customers behind it.

Helping to Develop Core Competencies. A focus on customer benefits is also *consistent with the seminal work on an organization's core competence*. Core competencies assist an organization to distinguish its brands from its competitors and to reduce costs more than competitors, thereby attaining a competitive advantage. According to the original article, "The Core Competency of the Corporation" by Prahalad and Hamel (1990), one crucial test of an organization's core competence is whether it "makes a significant contribution to the perceived customer benefits of the end product."[23]

As Exhibit 1.3 shows, brand benefits are important because they *help organizations ask relevant questions inspired by this benefit focus.*

EXHIBIT 1.3. Summary: How a Focus on Benefits Helps Organizations and Guides Marketing Decision-Making

Why Focus on Brand Benefits?	Relevant Questions Organizations Might Ask
A benefit focus is customer-focused	What benefits do (might) my customers want?
A benefit focus makes organizations' jobs easier	How can thinking about benefits affect how I segment markets, choose target customers, position my brand, and execute on my positioning?
Market	
A benefit focus helps organizations avoid marketing myopia	Am I thinking about my market broadly enough—outside the traditional areas where I compete?
A benefit focus helps organizations anticipate competitors	Am I thinking broadly enough about my competitors?
A benefit focus provides a clear view of new growth opportunities	Can I see new opportunities for growth (inside and outside the traditional areas in which I compete)?
Product	
A benefit focus helps organizations develop new product ideas	Are there new product ideas we can come up with based on benefits?
A benefit focus helps organizations understand shocks and trends	Is the importance people place on benefits dependent on shocks and trends?

Why Focus on Brand Benefits?	Relevant Questions Organizations Might Ask
Organizational	
A benefit focus helps organizations financially	How can I show the financial impact of marketing?
A benefit focus provides a lens for big data and AI	How can I make sense of results from big data or AI?
A benefit focus helps an organization develop core competencies	How do a gain a lasting advantage over competitors?

WHAT DO WE MEAN BY "CUSTOMERS"?

Throughout this chapter we've used the term "customer," and here we want to clarify what we mean by it. Our use of **customer** refers to individuals or groups of people (e.g., families or organizations) who are considering the purchase or use of whatever is being marketed. We focus on the consideration of whatever is being marketed as opposed to the final choice of a particular brand because customers typically evaluate brands in a competitive context where they assess which of multiple potential brands provides the benefits they want. Marketers' first job (beyond gaining awareness of their brand) is to get their brand into a consideration set of potential brands the customer is considering for purchase. From this consideration set, ultimately one and sometimes several brands are chosen. Benefits continue to play a strong role in the final purchase decision.

Because they are considering which brand to purchase or use, a customer could be a prospective customer, not necessarily a current customer. Also, depending on the situation, a customer could be an individual, such as a particular consumer or an individual voter in a political environment, a specific donor in a nonprofit context, or specific individual within a business-to-business environment. But the customer could also include smaller (e.g., couples or families) or larger (e.g., political groups, governments, or organizations) groups of people.

When the customer is an individual person, our focus is on the benefits that person is looking for. If the customer is a slightly larger group, like a couple, then the focus is more on the benefits wanted by the group. Similarly, when the customer is a family, your focus should be on the family. When the customer is a company or division of a company, your focus should be on the company or division. You will see examples of this, especially for B2B companies, throughout this book.

PLAYBOOK RULE #1

A focus on the benefits that customers want in a brand helps both customers and organizations.

After reading this chapter we hope you appreciate that focusing on customer benefits has many advantages for your organization. The main action point for you and your organization is to identify the benefits that customers in your market want. In appendix A, we explain how you can identify the benefits that customers in your market want. But before moving on, let's summarize the main points of this chapter.

KEY TAKEAWAYS

1. Benefits refer to the desirable outcomes that customers want from the product. Benefits are distinct from, but related to, product features and customer pain and goals.
2. There are three broad categories of benefits: functional, experiential, and symbolic.
3. Benefits help organizations in ways beyond merely being customer focused. They help organizations avoid marketing myopia, anticipate potential new competitors, identify new growth opportunities, develop new product ideas, build brand equity, and understand the impact of shocks and trends, and provide a lens through which strategic and tactical marketing decisions can be made.

KNOW *YOUR BRAND'S* BENEFITS

In the last chapter, we discussed why focusing on customer benefits is vital for your organization. This chapter explains why organizations should focus on brands. Indeed, no matter what you sell (products, services, experiences, ideas, or something else), everything that is marketed is a brand. By focusing on brands, the ideas in this book are applicable to any organization that does marketing.

Customers have perceptions (also called beliefs) about what benefits a brand offers. These perceptions are organized in customers' memory based on what they know about the brand from personal experience or what they've learned about it from your company, word of mouth, advertising, social media, influencers, public relations, and more.

Organizations have much to gain by thinking about benefits as the thing that truly makes their brand tick. Later in this chapter, we'll show how you can assess brand benefit perceptions using a perceptual map. Such maps illuminate how customers view your brand relative to your competitors' brands. As we explore in chapter four, perceptual maps are critical when positioning a brand and differentiating it from competitors. In fact, without a perceptual map, you'll have no idea whether customers perceive your brand in the way you want them to.

EVERYTHING MARKETED IS A BRAND

Let's take a step back and clarify why we want you to think about brands, not products. One crucial reason is that while almost everything that is marketed is a brand, only some brands are products (see Exhibit 2.1). Other brands are services, organizations, nonprofits, places, people, and so on. As a result, the term "product" is limiting. Because we focus on brands, the ideas in this book apply to everything that is marketed, not just products.

EXHIBIT 2.1. Almost Everything That Is Marketed Is a Brand

Types	Example Brands
Products	iPhone, Coca-Cola, Toyota Prius, Snickers
Services	UPS, Verizon, Wells Fargo, Hilton Hotels
Ingredients	Morton Salt, Intel, Pillsbury flour
Companies	Amazon, Google, Siemens, Starbucks
Nonprofits	Girl Scouts of the USA, American Heart Association, YMCA, Harvard University
Retailers	Trader Joe's, Nordstrom, Petco, Costco
Platforms	Airbnb, Yelp, Instagram, YouTube

Types	Example Brands
Media	*New York Times*, CNN, *Vogue*, NPR
Ideas	#MeToo, Black Lives Matter
Places	Bermuda, Gettysburg, the Metropolitan Museum of Art
NGOs	Doctors Without Borders, Amnesty International, Greenpeace, World Wildlife Fund
Organizations	American Democratic Party, National Football League
Charities	United Way, Salvation Army, Catholic Charities, Habitat for Humanity
Experiences	Spirit Rock, Shen Yun, Consumer Electronics Show
Utilities	Southern California Gas, Atmos Energy
People/ Influencers	Meryl Streep, Taylor Swift, Michael Jordan, Prince Harry, Vlad and Niki, Kylie Jenner

Some brands are combinations of the types shown in Exhibit 2.1. For example, Morton Salt is both an ingredient and a product; Starbucks is a retail establishment, service, place, and ingredient. If your organization markets a single product or service, your organization name is your brand. Even if you think you do not have a brand, you do. Even store brands like Safeway's "Signature SELECT" or CVS's own generic alternative to Tylenol is a brand. If you think that branding is irrelevant to you and your company, you are wrong. While, from your viewpoint, what you offer may be a product, from a customer's viewpoint it's a brand. Focusing on the brand and its benefits are the keys to success in the marketplace, because brands are essential to organizations and customers.

BRANDS ARE ESSENTIAL TO ORGANIZATIONS

Another important reason to focus on brands is that brands affect the organization's economic viability.[1] Organizations earn revenue and profits when customers purchase brands (Exhibit 2.2). Marketing activities are often organized around brands. Marketing budgets are set around brands and allocated to decisions about spending for brand name decisions, packaging, communications, distribution, web activities, and more. In B2B organizations, sales and sales pitches focus on brands. For these reasons, various organizations provide rankings of brands. This includes *Forbes*'s Most Valuable Brands,[2] Morning Consult's Most Trusted Brands,[3] and Interbrand's Best Global Brands,[4] among others. Given the importance of brands, it is not surprising that branding is often a top management priority.

And whereas the product can change and evolve, brands can endure over time. Some brands (like Ivory, Morton Salt, Tiffany & Co., American Express, Jack Daniel's, Coca-Cola, and Heinz) have been on the US market for over a hundred years. Although some of these brands offer more products today than when they first appeared the brands themselves have survived trends, shocks, population changes, cultural changes, leadership changes, and more.

Strong brands also provide barriers to entry for competitors, as is true with Walmart and Amazon, whose brand strength makes it difficult for new brands to compete successfully. Strong brands also command greater trade support and earn higher margins and greater customer loyalty.[5] Strong brands are generally less vulnerable to marketing crises. Strong brands also facilitate brand alliances, licensing opportunities, and co-branding options, as when two brands come together to market a new entity. They also facilitate brand extensions, as when a brand name that was used on one product (e.g., Heinz ketchup) is used on a new product (e.g., Heinz relish). These opportunities enhance the brand's growth potential.

EXHIBIT 2.2. Brands Are Essential to Organizations and Customers

From the Organization's Perspective
• The word "brand" accommodates most marketing entities (see Exhibit 2.1)
• Marketing activities are often organized around brands
• Brands earn revenue and profits for companies
• Salespeople sell brands
• Brands can endure over time (while products might not)
• Brand identification creates a barrier to entry for competitors by forcing new entrants to spend heavily to overcome customer loyalty[8]
• Brands enhance opportunities for growth
• Brands provide barriers to competition
• Brands influence employee motivation and retention
From the Customer's Perspective
• Customers talk to each other about brands (face-to-face and online)
• Customers make choices based on brands (brand choice)
• Customers can become attached to and admire brands (brand attachment, brand admiration)
• Customers can become loyal to brands (brand loyalty) and serve as brand advocates
• The brand name is an organizing device for representing customers' thoughts, feelings, and experiences with the marketing entity (brand image)

Given their experiences with brands, customers sometimes choose to work for strong brands; a factor that reduces employee acquisition costs. To illustrate, a recent study found that employees who worked for brands that empowered, excited, and inspired them worked harder, took more responsibility for, and were more committed to continue their work for the brand.[6] Employees who feel this way about the brands they work for are less likely to leave the company, reducing talent loss. Retaining valued employees has become a significant priority for organizations, particularly recently, as studied by the Fast Company Impact Council.[7]

BRANDS ARE IMPORTANT TO CUSTOMERS

Brands are also vital to customers. Customers talk to each other about brands and make choices based on brands.[9] Customers can develop strong and positive feelings toward brands, so much so that they become emotionally attached to them. Brand attachment builds brand loyalty and encourages customers to advocate on behalf of the brand.[10] Finally, as we explain next, customers organize what they know about the marketplace around brands.

The Brand Is a Set of (Benefit) Associations

A brand name represents the associations customers have in their memory about that brand and its benefits.[11] Marketing tries to build the associations customers have with a brand through the brand name, advertising, packaging, logos, product design, pricing, employee uniforms, encounters with employees, and customers' brand experiences. Ideally, these associations focus on the benefits of the brand. But customers' associations and the benefits that they link with the brand are also based on what they learn or hear about from others (such as brand users, competitors, influencers, the media, stock analysts, investors, and brand detractors). Notably, if customers are unaware of the brand, they have no associations linked to it in memory. (We return to this issue in chapter eight, when we talk about ways to enhance brand awareness.)

Some associations about brand benefits are thoughts, such as *perceptions or beliefs* about the brand's benefits, what the brand stands for, and what makes it different from other brands. Others are *emotions* about how the brand's benefits make customers feel (such as excited, nostalgic, secure, inspired). Still others are in the form of anticipated or remembered *experiences* with the brand, and what it was like to encounter the brand and its benefits.[12]

Some associations are *strong*, meaning that they are remembered automatically when one hears the brand name, whereas others are *weak* in their linkage with the brand. Brand associations become stronger the more vivid they are, the more often customers encounter this association when they use the brand, and the more frequently they hear this association from others. Customers regard some associations as *positive* (good from the customer's perspective); others are *negative* (bad from the customer's perspective). Some associations are *distinctive,* or unique from the customer's perspective, whereas others are less distinctive. For example, when it comes to art supplies, the brand Liquitex markets itself as distinctive by formulating their paints, sprays, inks, and mediums such that they work together seamlessly. The "brand" is a combination of their customers' thoughts, emotions, and experiences with these supplies, which have varying strengths, valences (positivity), and distinctiveness.

Consider the potential perceptions, emotions, and experiences a hypothetical customer might link to the Peloton brand (see Exhibit 2.3).

Assume this customer is a non-user, so their associations to this brand come from Peloton's ads and what other people have told them. This customer associates Peloton with being pricey (a negative belief). On the other hand, the workouts involve videos on demand (a positive belief), and the exercises seem to be fun (a positive emotion). This customer also associates Peloton with working out from home (a positive anticipated experience). The workouts are perceived to be intense, which is slightly negative for this customer since they are not in good shape (a negative perception). On the other hand, they think it might be a good idea for them to challenge themselves (a positive emotion).

EXHIBIT 2.3. Hypothetical Customer's Associations Linked to the Peloton Brand

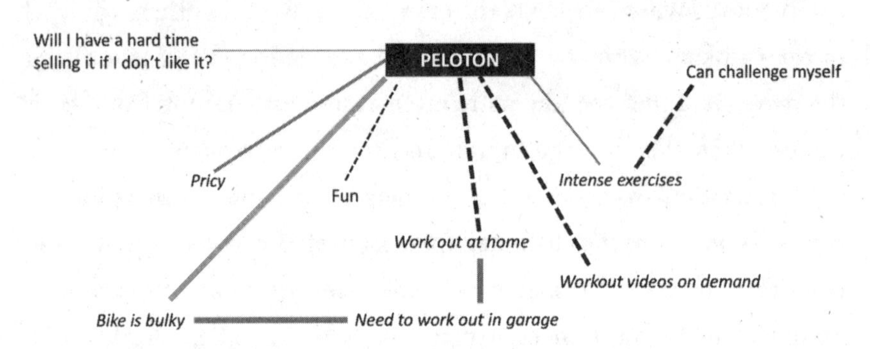

Solid = negative association
Dotted = positive association
Thickness of line = salience of association
Italic = thoughts
Nonitalic = emotions

This customer also believes that the Peloton bike is bulky (a negative belief) and that their partner would not want them to keep it in the living room or bedroom. So, they would need to store it in the garage and work out there (also a negative anticipated experience). They also worry that if they don't like it, they might have a hard time selling it (a negative anticipated experience).

Some people use "brand image" to refer to the cluster of associations customers link to the brand. Note that some of these associations related to the benefits of Peloton (those with thick lines in Exhibit 2.3) are highly top of mind (i.e., salient), whereas others are less so (those with thin lines). Some are thoughts; others are connected to emotions (like anticipating it being fun, wanting to challenge oneself, being anxious about selling it). As a result of these associations, this customer has a slightly negative or somewhat ambivalent perspective on the brand. Notable as well is that none of the positive and salient associations linked to Peloton are unique or distinctive.

The associations customers link to a brand may or may not be true of the brand.

Note that the associations customers link to a brand may or may not be true of the brand. For example, the customer in Exhibit 2.3 may perceive that Peloton bikes are hard to sell should they choose to resell them, but this belief may not be correct. Other associations are inferred based on what customers know about the world. For example, the customer in Exhibit 2.3 may infer that because Peloton is expensive, it must have a great warranty, an inference that may or may not be correct.

What associations come to mind when you think about Starbucks, Doctors Without Borders, the LA Rams, and Harry Potter? Which associations are salient, positive, or distinctive? Strong brands have benefit associations that are strong, positive, and highly distinctive.[13] What about the brand you market? Do customers in your market have strong (easily recallable), positive, and distinctive associations linked to your brand? If you're not sure, this is where a good focus group or survey can help identify gaps or messaging opportunities.

Brand Perceptions Affect Purchase Decisions

One implication of the discussion in the previous section is that positive, salient, and distinctive associations influence customers' purchase and usage decisions. We argue that some of the most important perceptions reflect customers' beliefs about the functional, experiential, and symbolic *benefits* of the brand; that is, what it can do for them, and how it makes their lives better. When customers view brand benefits as positive and essential, they will develop a positive brand attitude. Academic consumer research has validated that customers' beliefs about important benefits influence their brand attitudes and intentions to spend money on the brand.[14] When these important benefits are realized through their experiences with the brand, their brand attitudes will become stronger and more resistant to change.[15] This is particularly true when the brand outperforms competitors on these benefits. But even if competitors come up with something better, the fact that customers' attitudes are resistant to change means that they will stay with the brand that they already like. The relationship between favorable brand attitudes and purchase intentions is also influenced by how other people talk about the brand. For example, if credible others speak favorably about the brand, customers are motivated to listen to what they have to say.[16]

Regrettably, brands can also fall short in providing the benefits that customers want, which means that their attitudes are weakly held and not very favorable, so purchase intentions are low. For example, a recent study of US and Canadian consumers found that approximately two-thirds of the study's participants believed that the brands that they transact with on digital platforms need to up their game in improving customer experiences online. Over three-fourths of consumers said they were willing to spend money on brands that provided better customer experiences, while half of millennials and Gen Z respondents indicated a willingness to share personal data for improved customer experiences online.[17] Brands that address such issues can do much better with customers.

CUSTOMERS' PERCEPTIONS OF BRANDS AND THEIR BENEFITS

You can visualize how customers perceive a brand and its benefits by developing a perceptual map.

Perceptual Maps

A **perceptual map** is a visual representation of how customers in the market perceive the benefits of your brand relative to competitors' brands. Perceptual maps are the only way to see how customers currently view your brand's position in the market.

From customers' perspectives, a perceptual map depicts where brands in the market stand in providing certain benefits at a point in time. To see how this works, let's examine a perceptual map of several brands in the home exercise market.

According to the BBC, home exercise equipment is not a new idea.[18] Gustav Ernst, an orthopedic machinist based in London, invented the first portable home gym, which he described in a book in 1861. Today, home exercise equipment has added innovations and benefits like sharing one's performance data and providing status identity (a sense of prestige) to users in the exercise arena.

We chose this industry because we are writing this book in 2022, while still in the throes of the COVID pandemic. At the start of the pandemic, the home exercise market boomed as people stayed home and gyms closed. Peloton's stock went up more than 400 percent in 2020. Some observers thought this market would continue after the pandemic receded,[19] even though the financial results of home exercise companies were deteriorating.[20] As a result, this is a market in flux, with a lot of potential for competitive upsets with well-applied brand benefits thinking.

A perceptual map is the only way to see how customers currently view your brand's position in the market.

We began investigating this industry by holding informal focus groups with a sample of students in a marketing MBA class. Using the techniques discussed in appendix A of this book, we identified six benefits that customers in this market want. They include not only functional benefits (convenience) but also symbolic benefits (e.g., the ability to share performance data and create status identity) and experiential benefits (e.g., the home exercise equipment is visually pleasing and the home exercise equipment provides enjoyment/entertainment). For this exercise we focused on only three brands in the market: Peloton, Lululemon Studio Mirror, and Nordic Track. Please note that if we were doing a perceptual map in earnest, we would include most of the brands on the market and would have spent much more time deriving the benefits. Nonetheless, this data provides a useful example of how a perceptual map works.

In August 2022, after our focus groups, we enlisted a panel of about five hundred customers who exercised at least three times per week. We asked respondents to use a 10-point scale to describe how strongly each brand provides each benefit (1 = not at all; 10 = a great deal), which is presented on the vertical axis along with their perceptions of the price of each brand. Exhibit 2.4 shows the results, based on the means from the survey. Note that for ease of presentation, a shorthand version of the benefit is indicated along the horizontal axis (e.g., "Visually Pleasing" for the benefit "the home exercise equipment is visually pleasing").

EXHIBIT 2.4. Illustrative Perceptual Map Showing Perceptions of Three Brands on Multiple Benefits

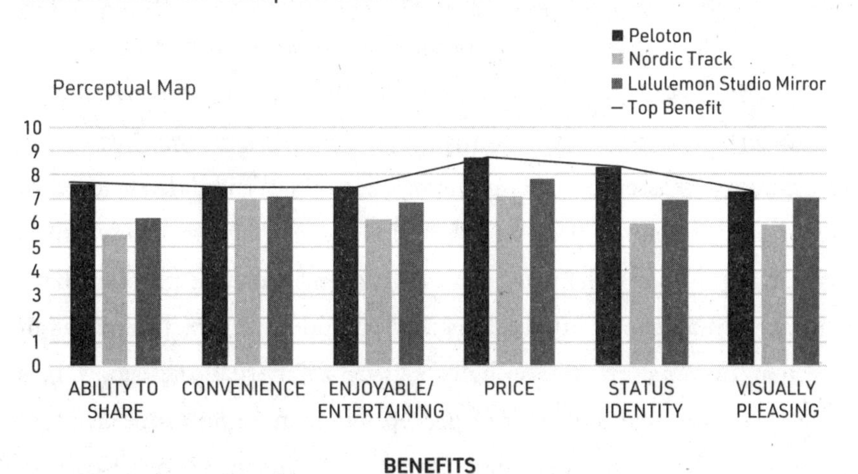

In this illustrative case, Peloton dominates the other brands on the benefits, but is perceived to have the highest price. In a sense, Peloton's

dominance is consistent with how much brand advertising Peloton did during the first couple of years of the pandemic.[21] You can see how close the different brands are on the benefit of convenience and how far apart they are on the benefit of status identity and the ability to share their performance data with others. But you can also see that perceptions of the Lululemon Studio Mirror are close to those of Peloton on many of the benefits.

One thing you might notice is that the map in Exhibit 2.4 differs from a "classic" perceptual map, which is often shown in two dimensions. The two-dimensional maps arise from situations in which analysts focus on features, or highly correlated characteristics, rather than benefits. Since a product or service can have many features, it's necessary to "reduce" the data, using fancy methods like multidimensional scaling, into two-dimensional space. But with benefits, it's not typically necessary to do such manipulations. Additionally, when you don't reduce the data down to two dimensions, the results are more informative, because they allow you to see where your brand falls not just on two dimensions, but on all the benefits that customers in the market want. The data set used to generate the map in Exhibit 2.5 had seventeen attributes, which is why it required a reduction into two dimensions. The problem with the two-dimensional approach is that you do not know the names of the map dimensions, so you have to infer what the dimension labels might be. Because traditional perceptual maps emphasize product features and don't label what the dimensions mean, we don't recommend this two-dimensional approach.

EXHIBIT 2.5. Perceptual Map in Two Dimensions *(Produced by Enginius software, DecisionPro, Inc.)*

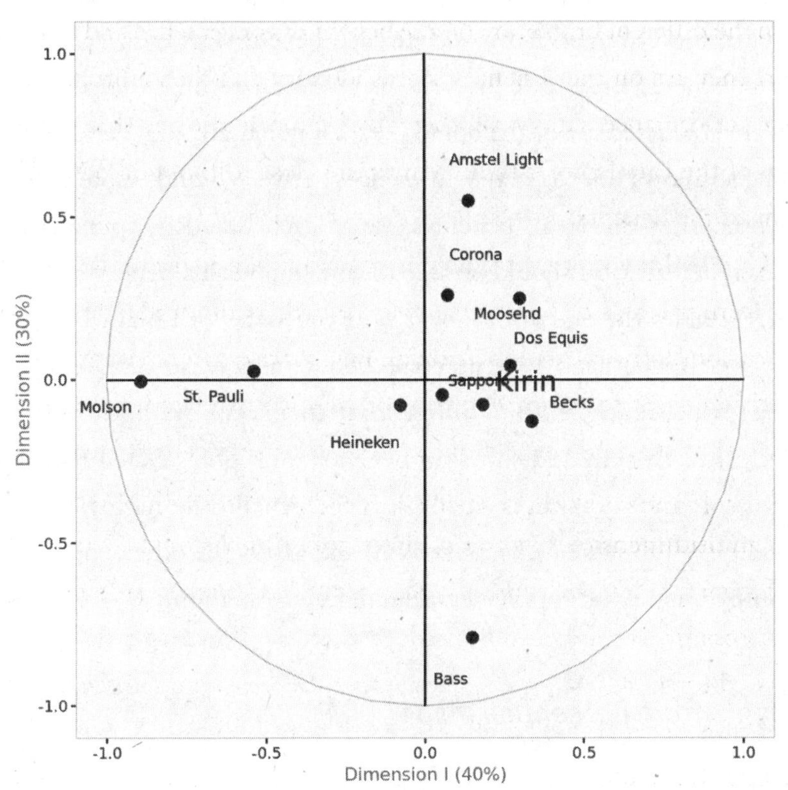

How to Create Perceptual Maps

Readers unfamiliar with perceptual maps might ask how to create them when using benefits. The process is relatively simple. First, use the laddering approach described next to identify the benefits that customers want. Laddering is a method of interviewing customers to obtain the benefits they use when making judgements and decisions. Laddering typically begins by identifying what attributes of a product customers find important and then linking these essential attributes to the benefits that drive customers' decisions (see appendix A to learn more about laddering). Then ask a representative sample of customers to evaluate how strongly they associate each benefit with each brand. It's best to use a response scale that lets customers assess how *much* the benefits are characteristic of the brand (i.e., 1 = not at all; 10 = very much). Doing so allows you to see the differences between brands more clearly. By comparing the mean benefit score of each brand in your market for each benefit, you should be able to come up with a perceptual map that resembles the one in Exhibit 2.4. If you start with many benefits, ask yourself whether all are necessary. Some may be so similar that it doesn't make much sense to differentiate them. For example, in hand lotion, smooth skin and soft skin benefits are highly related (smooth skin is soft and soft skin is smooth). If the benefits are highly related, you might eliminate one (smooth skin) and assess the other (soft skin), because assessing both provides redundant information.

Insights from Perceptual Maps

Perceptual maps provide several insights to marketers. First, perceptual maps allow you to see how customers perceive your brand relative to competitors' brands. If your brand and another brand are perceived to be similar on the benefits they provide, they are likely to be direct competitors.

This insight might have implications for how you wish to position your product, as we explain in chapter four. For example, you may want to differentiate your brand from your closest competitor, particularly on a benefit that customers regard as important.

Second, perceptual maps will reveal any places where no competitor is currently competing, or where no competitor has competed successfully, as when all brands are low on a given benefit. (Notably, this may be the case because no customers are interested in that benefit or combination of benefits.)

Third, a perceptual map should also reveal how far away you are from being perceived as the best; that is, how far you are away from what we call the "nirvana point" that customers in the segment want. For example, in Exhibit 2.4, the brands are perceived as just above average on most benefits. None has achieved a score of "10" on how much the brand provides that benefit.

EXHIBIT 2.6. Insights from Perceptual Maps

• Allows you to see how customers perceive your brand relative to competitors' brands
• Reveals any places where no competitor is currently competing, or where no competitor has competed successfully
• Reveals how far away you are from being perceived as the best
• Helps you spot new opportunities

A perceptual map can also help you notice completely new opportunities. The beer industry provides a classic example of this. Beer has been around forever. So, you would think that by 1970 beer organizations would know everything there was to know about customers and beer. But a perceptual map, based on two benefits, produced insights that changed the industry.

The perceptual map revealed that no beer was perceived as being in between bitter and mild. Instead, they were either bitter or mild. The taste factor (an experiential benefit) was treated as two discrete categories as opposed to a continuous dimension. Additionally, no beer was perceived as light (rather than heavy). In 1975, because of the perceptual map, Miller launched their new "Miller Lite" brand as offering new benefits. The brand's "Tastes Great! . . . Less Filling!" tagline and its copy—which noted, "Lite Beer from Miller: Everything you always wanted in a beer. And less"—were designed to highlight why customers should buy Miller Lite. Miller's ability to successfully position the brand in the minds of customers has made this ad campaign one of the best in history.

Some observers[22] have drawn the wrong lesson from the campaign. They believe Miller created a whole new category of light beer. But what Miller did was understand the perceptions in the beer market and position themselves accordingly. The *result* was a new category based on a new understanding the market, which a perceptual map gave them.

CUSTOMER PERCEPTIONS VERSUS ORGANIZATIONS' EFFORTS

So now we know what a brand is from your customer's perspective. However, customers' perceptions of the brand in terms of its benefits may or may not be the perceptions you intended customers to have. For this reason, we differentiate between the brand as customers perceive it and the brand as organizations wish it to be perceived. (We return to the latter issue in chapter four, when we talk about positioning statements. It's like a two-sided market, and you need to think on both the customer and the organizational sides of the market when focusing on positioning.) We raise this issue because we often hear from organizations that they have positioned their product without ever thinking about how customers actually perceive it.

Let's provide an example of thinking this way in a political campaign. The candidate (i.e., your organization) is trying to position themselves with voters (i.e., customers) in order to win an election (i.e., sales). The candidate goes on TV and podcasts, gives stump speeches, etc., to position themselves in a certain way. How they position themselves can be quite different than the way voters perceive the candidate. For example, a mayoral candidate (a political brand) might run on a platform of solving homelessness. Even if this is a major part of the platform, voters still might not perceive the candidate as being able to solve this problem, and an awareness of their perceptions is necessary for adjusting the candidate's image.

Customers' perceptions of the brand in terms of its benefits may or may not be the perceptions you intended customers to have.

WHICH BENEFITS ARE MOST IMPORTANT?

From the organization's perspective, the brand represents what promises they make to customers about the brand. Once you have a perceptual map, you will be tempted to decide what changes you need to make to your brand and messaging to start making promises. But perceptions of how strongly a brand provides each benefit is only one part of the story. The other part is how important these benefits are to customers.

To give you a feel for this, we start with a basic observation: whereas some customers might want a brand to max out on all benefits, no brand on the market does so. Instead, some brands are better than others on certain benefits. So, customers need to make tradeoffs—that is, decide which benefits are most important to them. For example, imagine that you are a customer in the market for home exercise equipment. In Exhibit 2.7, allocate 100 points such that you give the most points to those benefits that are most important to you.

EXHIBIT 2.7. Making Benefit Trade-Offs

Benefit	Benefit Importance (How Much Do Customers Want It) (0 to 100-point scale)
Visual Pleasantness (*Experiential*)	
Social Sharing of Data (*Functional and Symbolic*)	
Enjoyment/Entertainment of Use (*Experiential*)	
Status Conferred (*Symbolic*)	
Convenience of Setup and Use (*Functional*)	
Total Points:	100 Points

You are unlikely to distribute these 100 points equally across the different benefits. You will more likely do what most humans do—you make trade-offs, awarding more points to those benefits you care most about. There are likely to be clusters of customers in the market who differ in what's most important to them (i.e., people in the same cluster want one set of benefits most while those in a different cluster care about a different set of benefits).

These clusters are called benefit segments, which we describe in chapter three, where we begin to implement the ideas we have been discussing. Knowing what customers care most about also helps you develop a positioning statement that articulates these promised benefits (chapter four) for a target segment. This positioning statement needs to be subjected to several stress tests to ensure it is credible (chapter five) and defensible in the market (chapter six). Marketing activities should support the positioning statement such that the promised benefits of a brand are delivered to customers (chapter eight).

The perceptions of how strongly brands provide each benefit are only one part of the story. The other part is how important these benefits are to customers.

In some cases, customers are unfamiliar with the brand. Or perhaps they have heard the brand name but can't say anything about what it stands for and what benefits it provides to customers. In such cases, marketers need to build brand-name recall or recognition and establish brand knowledge. We discuss these issues in chapter eight.

PLAYBOOK RULE # 2

Customers perceive brands in terms of the benefits they provide compared with competitors' brands.

It is crucial to think about your brand and its benefits vis-à-vis competitors. The main action point for you, the reader, is to create a perceptual map of you and your competitors' brands on the various benefits. With it, you will understand how you are currently positioned in the market and can also gain an understanding of how you compare to your competitors. Before moving on, let's summarize the main points.

KEY TAKEAWAYS

1. All marketed entities are brands, but only some brands are products. Services, organizations, people, nonprofits, places, celebrities, and influencers are just some of the marketing entities that are brands.
2. Marketers can develop a perceptual map to assess how strongly customers associate their brand and competitors' brands with the benefits that customers in the market want. Perceptual maps provide insights to marketers such as who their closest competitors are, how much they are perceived as being strong on all benefits, and whether customers perceive their brand in the way they intend.
3. Customers make trade-offs in terms of which benefits are most important to them. This is a fundamental human process and naturally leads to benefit segmentation, and a set of marketing decisions that follow from deciding which segment to target. The following chapters illustrate how.

SEGMENT ON BENEFITS

We know that customers want the benefits that brands give them, and they choose one brand over another because of its benefits. But do all customers in your markets want the same benefits? The short answer is generally no. Typically, there are groups of customers for whom certain benefits are most important. For example, the next time you go shopping, look at the options in the toothpaste aisle. One group of customers cares most about the symbolic benefits of white, bright teeth. Another group cares most about experiential benefits like minty taste. A different group cares most about the functional benefits of decay prevention and avoiding plaque and gum disease. We use the word "care" to refer to the degree to which a group of customers wants a benefit or how important that benefit is to them.

In this chapter, we emphasize segmenting your market based on customers' benefits preferences, which gives you a view of the benefits playing field. We'll illustrate benefit segmentation and indicate why segmenting markets based on benefits offers a much better strategic view of the market than any other segmentation system. We also show how organizations can segment their markets based on benefits.

BENEFIT SEGMENTATION

Market segmentation is essentially a classification system in which you break up the market into groups of customers, such that people in the same group are similar to one another and different from people in other groups.

With benefit segmentation, the market is classified into distinct groups (or segments), such that customers in the same segment view the same set of benefits as important (i.e., they make the same trade-offs with respect to benefits). Customers in other segments, meanwhile, view other benefits as important, as in the toothpaste example at the start of this chapter. Market segmentation based on benefits has long history in marketing.[1] Indeed, as originally defined, the term "market segmentation" emphasized benefit segmentation, rather than segmenting by vertical, industry, demographic, or other ways. Benefit segmentation is equally applicable to business-to-consumer (B2C) as well as business-to-business (B2B) markets. Indeed, any market can be segmented based on what benefits customers regard as important.

Illustrating Benefit Segmentation

Let's illustrate the idea of benefit segmentation in the document management industry, a B2B setting. The term "document management" describes a system that captures and stores electronic documents (PDFs, digital images, word processing files, etc.). All types and sizes of companies, from small businesses to large corporations, use these systems to organize, secure, and classify company documents and make them easy to access, edit, and share. These systems first appeared in the 1980s and have improved over the years, particularly in terms of security and ease of use. Still, companies today need specialists to manage them. A company in this industry contracted with us to help them position their document management product in the large corporate market, which includes several major competitors. The first step was to identify the benefits that customers in the market care about, using methods presented in appendix A. The next step was to segment the market.

Our work with the company showed that the market could be broken up into the four benefit segments depicted in Exhibit 3.1. The exhibit lists the benefits each segment wanted most, organized in terms of how important they were to customers within that segment.

EXHIBIT 3.1. Example Benefit Segmentation

Most Important Benefits, in Order of Importance			
Segment 1	**Segment 2**	**Segment 3**	**Segment 4**
Ease of use Customized retrieval Control over distribution	Ability to manage multiple data types Customized retrieval Compatibility	Cost Compatibility Ease of use	Customized retrieval Compatibility Ease of use

Note: We gathered importance weights on nine benefits (and price); the top three in each segment are depicted here.

All the benefits that customers wanted in this market were functional, but customers in each segment found different benefits to be most important. For example, customers in Segment 3 cared most about cost, compatibility with their current document system, and ease of use. In contrast, customers in Segment 2 cared most about whether they could manage multiple data types and customize their retrieval. Why don't the customers in the four segments regard the same benefits as important? That's because they are making trade-offs—as we explained in chapter two.

After segmenting the market, the company was able to determine which segment they should target (a topic we discuss in the next chapter). The document management company we worked with ultimately decided to target Segment 2 based on their analysis of competitors, a perceptual map, and their company's capabilities. Because they knew what benefits were most important to these target customers, they had insights into what their messaging should look like. In short, their communication messages would emphasize their product's ability to manage multiple data types, its customized retrieval capabilities, and its compatibility, since customers in Segment 2 cared most about those benefits.

Benefit Segmentation and Competition

Based on the market segmentation analysis, we helped the client determine which competitors were aligned with each segment. The analysis showed that no one competitor was strongly associated with Segment 1, and that three competitors seemed to have products that focused mostly on customers in Segments 2, 3, and 4, respectively. One competitor seemed to straddle the four segments and was not clearly associated with any one segment in particular. By focusing on Segment 2, the company had a better idea about which competitors were direct (i.e., their closest) competitors. Since their competitors were unlikely to know these same ideas about benefit segmentation and competition at the level of the market, the client had a better strategic view of the market and how to approach it over time than their competitors.

Finally, we helped the client identify who the buyers were in each of the four segments. For example, the people who wanted the benefits associated with Segment 4 were large corporate law firms, while those who wanted the benefits associated with Segment 2 were companies with high-end office automation. In this situation, the types of companies, or context (e.g., high-end office automation), represent "descriptors" of each segment.

For another B2B example, consider the case of companies that want machine identity protection. Simply put, these are the protected keys and certificates on computers that keep your company's networks secure. We helped a client in this industry segment its market too. We identified six benefit segments.

As we determined how to segment the company's benefits, we considered the financial and reputational harm that a security breach would cause in some companies' networks. You know these companies because they show up in the news all the time. For example, in 2012, a breach at LinkedIn affected 700 million users. In 2018, a breach at Marriott Starwood Hotels and Resorts affected 500 million guests. For companies like these, the benefit of "world-class reliability" protection is extremely important. For other companies, where a breach is unwanted but wouldn't cause significant harm, world-class reliability is nice to have, but the benefits of reasonable price and ease of use would be more important. They would trade off world-class reliability for a lower price. By understanding which benefits customers in each segment found important, our client company was in a much better position to see (a) the market as a whole, (b) which competitors were targeting which segments, (c) which segment would be a viable option for the client, and (d) how to reach customers in that segment.

Organizations rarely segment their market in such a systematic way. Indeed, some organizations fail to segment their market at all, and instead attempt to appeal to everybody. Doing so wastes precious resources, since not everybody regards the benefits that you are selling as important. If you don't segment the market on benefits, who would your salespeople focus on? What would your messaging be? You would see competitors, of course, but you would have no idea which were the closest to you and which segments other competitors were targeting.

Other organizations do attempt to segment the market, but they use other, less successful segmentation systems, which can cause their own sets of problems, as we show next.

OTHER SEGMENTATION SYSTEMS

Instead of focusing directly on the benefits customers want, most marketing books, websites, consultants, and even marketing professors promote an enormous array of ways to segment a market. Indeed, one article on the web identifies fifty-one such ways.[2] In essence, these approaches use things other than benefits to break up the B2C market. Chances are, one or more of these segmentation systems will look very familiar to you. In our view, it

It is inaccurate to use these other segmentation systems, because they are not based on what customers want or find important.

is inaccurate to use these other segmentation systems, because they are not based on what customers want or find important. Does this mean that all the other ways people have classified a market are irrelevant? Not at all. As we explain in detail later, we can use these other systems to *describe* the customers in each benefit segment.

Common Market Segmentation Systems in Consumer Markets

Over the years, a wide variety of alternative market segmentation systems have been offered. In this section we list these systems and explain their limitations.

Geographics. One segmentation system focuses on geographics, like population density (rural, urban, suburban), or state, country, or continent of residence. The claim is that people in different regions vary in what they want from brands. For example, customers in, say, a suburban district are thought to want something different from a brand than customers in an urban district. Some organizations sell their brand in a particular geographic area. For example, a winter athletic apparel company may focus on specific climate geographies. However, such an approach is about regional communication and the distribution of a brand in a geographic territory. It's not about the benefits that customers want, but rather about how your organization is marketing to a particular group (or class) of people.

Demographics. Another approach uses demographics to segment a market; for example, grouping the market by age (i.e., the 18–40, 41–60, and 60+ age groups), cohort (Gen Z, Gen X, baby boomers, etc.), income (<$25K, $25–50K, $51–75K, $100K+), marital status, family size, occupation, and more. Consider people in the millennial

EXHIBIT 3.2. Geographic and Demographic Approaches to Segmentation

Geographic Segmentation

1. State (California, Colorado, Texas)
2. Country (USA, Canada, Australia, India)
3. College (The University of Illinois, The New School, Santa Monica College)
4. County (Los Angeles County, Butte County)
5. Continent (Europe, the Americas, Africa, Asia)
6. Community (San Marcos Youth Master Plan)
7. Urban/rural
8. North/south region
9. Warm/cold areas
10. High-elevation/low-elevation areas

Demographic Segmentation

11. Age (21–29, 30–44, 44–59)
12. Race (Asian, Native Hawaiian)
13. Religion (Muslim, Buddhist, Christian)
14. Gender (women, men)
15. Family size (couple only, three family members)
16. Income ($40,000 USD, $40–50,000 USD)
17. Education (high school, university)
18. Ethnicity (Hispanic, Middle Eastern)
19. Housing style (ranch house, modernist)
20. Marital status (married, single, widowed)
21. Occupation (blue collar, white collar, trade)

and Gen Z cohorts. People in Gen Z were born between 1997 and 2012. Bloomberg calls some of the brands focusing on this cohort "Adorkables" as they "deftly target Gen Z by using jarring visual aesthetics and an authentic emotional appeals."[3] They include brands like Topicals (in the beauty industry), Flewd (in the self-care industry) and BEHAVE (in the snack food industry). Once again, this approach focuses on one class of potential customers, not the market as a whole and how customers' wants and values affect it. If these companies did segment the market on benefits, we are confident they would find many other non–Gen Z consumers who also want the experiential benefits of jarring visual aesthetics and an authentic emotional appeal, and many Gen Z customers who don't want these things at all.

Segmenting a market based on demographics might make sense if all members of a given age, income, or marital category want the same benefits. But often, this is not the case. Organizations typically use demographics because they can conveniently reach customer groups and appeal to them through advertising. But segmenting a market based on benefits and reaching customers in a particular segment are different.

Psychographics. You'll also read about segmentation systems based on psychographics, such as lifestyles, interests, religious beliefs, values, personality characteristics, etc. Again, these approaches might make sense if they reflect the benefits that customers want. However, psychographics are often better used to describe customers, not to segment the market. Moreover, psychographics need not map directly onto benefits. For example, knowing that certain people are "heavy users" of movie theaters gives you limited information about what benefits they would find important in the automotive market (or any other market, for that matter).

Behaviors. You'll also read about segmentation systems based on behaviors, such as the stage of the customer journey each customer is in (i.e., awareness, learning, consideration, purchase, or adoption), buyer status (new users, existing users, or former users), usage rate (heavy versus light users), loyalty status (loyal, nonloyal, or multi-brand loyal), and more. These groups might loosely map onto benefits. For example, heavy users of day-to-day items like household supplies likely regard (low) prices as important. But knowing that someone is a heavy user provides no insight into what other benefits they regard as important.

Media Habits and Time. You'll also read about segmentation systems based on media habits, like using different cable TV channels, radio, social media, newspapers, and search engines, as well as segmentation based on time, such as the season of the year, special events, and holidays. Once again, however, these classification systems don't describe what benefits that people want or how certain benefits are important to customers. People whose media habits involve watching nighttime news, for example, probably want the benefit of information and being in the know, along with other benefits, such as interesting visuals, credible reporting, and easy-to-understand content. But segmenting a market based on time of day is not synonymous with segmenting based on benefits.

EXHIBIT 3.3. Psychographic and Behavioral Approaches to Segmentation

Psychographic Segmentation

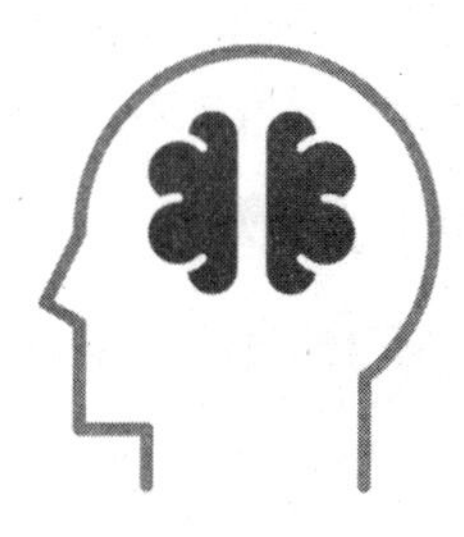

22. Class (working class, middle class)
23. Personality (outgoing, creative, serious)
24. Attitudes (hope, optimism, realism)
25. Lifestyles (healthy lifestyle, gluten-free lifestyle)
26. Special character traits (religious, adventurous)
27. Expectations (explicit, implicit)
28. Opinions (customers that rate the product with three stars, four stars, five stars)
29. Hobbies (reading, horse riding)
30. Interests (technology, fashion)

Behavioral Segmentation

31. Occasion (birthday, anniversary)
32. Buyer journey stage (awareness, consideration, decision stage)
33. Brand knowledge (none, some, strong knowledge)
34. Types of loyalty (no loyalty, inertia loyalty)
35. Price sensitivity (sensitive to price changes, not sensitive)
36. Shopping style (avoid shopping, enjoy shopping)
37. Usage rate (heavy, light)
38. User status (never, occasional, regular)

EXHIBIT 3.4. Media and Time Approaches to Segmentation

Media Segmentation

39. TV (cable TV, network TV, satellite TV)
40. Radio (satellite radio use, internet radio, local radio, national radio)
41. Social media (Facebook, Twitter, Instagram)
42. Newspapers (local, national, consumer magazine)
43. Internet search engine use (Google, Bing, Yahoo)

Time Segmentation

44. Seasons (winter, spring, summer, autumn)
45. Special events (Black Friday)
46. Holidays (Thanksgiving, Halloween)

A new and popular metric called the Cultural Insights Impact Measure aims to help brands access cultural relevance.[4] In multicultural marketing, the term "segment" describes culture-based groupings, such as Hispanic Americans, Asian Americans, etc. But unless customers in these culture-based groups all want the same benefits, they are not, in our view, benefit-based market segments.

Common Segmentation Systems in Business-to-Business Markets

Using classification systems to break up a market into segments is not unique to B2C markets. Allen recently attended a B2B Forrester conference and attended a session called "Finding Hidden Growth Opportunities: Turning Segmentation and Targeting into Treasure." When the Forrester presenters got to the segmentation part, they put up a table like that shown in Exhibit 3.5. In essence, attendees were informed that they could segment the market based on company size (e.g., large, medium, or small), industry (e.g., education, health care, apparel, automotive), industry growth rate (slow, moderate, or fast), and nineteen other classification systems. The upshot of the segmentation part of the presentation was essentially, "You figure it out."

EXHIBIT 3.5. Common Segmentation Systems in B2B Markets

Company size	Profitability
Industry or vertical marketing	Market position
Region	Revenue and sales models
Location	Geographic activities
Age or maturity	Indirect or direct customer
Technology systems used	Types of offerings
Buying center attributes	Organizational culture
Credit rating/debt	Technology adoption
Growth rate	Growth strategy
Types of employees	Corporate governance
Mission or purpose	

These days, a popular B2B focus for organizations is on "vertical marketing." Vertical marketing refers to targeting an industry, trade, profession, or some similar specific group. Example vertical groups include legal, education, health care, automotive, and finance markets, or a specific niche, such as staff members of universities. The idea is to offer products and services that are specialized to these customers in a specific vertical. When companies segment the market based on verticals, they immediately determine a target vertical and then go directly to personas, audience types, messaging, and stories without ever stopping to assess whether customers in each vertical want the same benefits and whether these benefits differ from those wanted by customers in different verticals.

PROBLEMS WITH NOT SEGMENTING THE MARKET ON BENEFITS

There are several problems with not segmenting the market on benefits. Exhibit 3.6 summarizes these problems.

The first problem of not segmenting the market on benefits, or not segmenting at all, is that you have no sense of the entire market and the competitive landscape. You also have limited understanding of how competitors are aligned with different segments. A benefit segmentation approach lets you see which segments competitors are focusing their efforts on, which segments are less crowded, and even segments where no competitor has entered. When you join benefit segmentation with a perceptual map, you also see how close or far you are from competitors in the eyes of customers in the market. Additionally, when segmenting on benefits, you see what customers really want, and you are in a better position to evaluate whether certain segments are more

EXHIBIT 3.6. Problems When You Don't Segment the Market by Benefits

Area of Problem	Problem
Market view and competitive landscape	You have little idea of how the market and the competitive landscape are structured.
Marketing communication	Marketing communications will be financially wasteful, and people will not know how to talk about your brand in a meaningful way.
Decision focus	The number of ways to segment the market will create indecision and confusion.
Explanatory power	These other approaches to segmentation do not predict actual purchase behavior very well.

attractive than others by virtue of their size, growth rates, and the number and size of competitors.

A second problem is that without segmenting on benefits, communications about your brand are not likely to resonate with customers, because they are not focused on what is meaningful to customers. Other segmentation schemes represent only very loose approximations of what people want. They may even have no bearing whatsoever on what people want. Thus, your communications will be financially wasteful.

A third problem is that the sheer number of approaches to market segmentation can lead to indecision among organizations about whether they have broken up their markets in a way that leads to the best customer insights. For example, should you segment the market by multiple criteria, such as TV type used, radio type used, and newspaper type read—or just one? If one, which one? So many different approaches to market classification can lead to decision paralysis, since organizations have no idea about which approach to follow. No wonder many companies resort to not segmenting the market at all or relying on other descriptions of customers to break up the market. Unfortunately, the word "segment," like the word "market," can mean any number of different things, confusing organizations in the process. For these reasons, it's not surprising that studies show that 85 percent of new product launches fail due to inadequate market segmentation.[5]

85 percent of new product launches fail due to inadequate market segmentation.

A fourth problem is that, as prior research finds, these other approaches to market segmentation show little difference in actual purchase behavior.[6] For example, differences in actual purchase behaviors between such geographic- and demographic-based segments are small. The same problem exists when using psychographics as bases for segmentation.[7] Because benefit segmentation directly maps into what customers want and what will motivate their purchase, you are much more likely to see effects on actual behavior.

Let's illustrate some of these problems with an example. Imagine that you are a "software as a service" (or SaaS) company. Your company sells a software product in the health care space, and you have been told to engage in vertical marketing. The verticals that the company focuses on are large health care plans and medical practices/doctors. It's highly likely that when you focus on the benefits of this market, the large health care plans are not monolithically interested in the same benefits, nor are the doctors and medical practices.

Assume that the company has not segmented the market on benefits. Consequently, you have no idea what benefits customers in each vertical care about, as Exhibit 3.7 shows. Thus, you don't know whether the verticals are distinct, meaning that you don't know if the customers in the large health care plan's vertical are different from doctors and medical practices in terms of the benefits they seek. Because you know nothing about what customers in these verticals want, all that you know about customers is that they are members of two customer groups. Because you lack information about these customers, you have no idea how to position your product in a way that will win them over. Any messaging that you do will likely be confusing and fail to connect with customers. This is an example of the first two points in Exhibit 3.6. Your messaging will be financially wasteful, and you have no real idea of the customer market. Moreover, any competitors will just be competitors for Vertical 1 or 2, without any sense of the whole market.

EXHIBIT 3.7. The Industry Perspective on Verticals

Segment	Vertical 1: Healthcare Plans	Vertical 2: Medical Practices/Doctors
What benefits do they care about?	?	?
Are the segments distinct in what they care about?	?	?
Is precise, unique, and defensible positioning possible?	No	No

But if you follow the benefit segmentation approach, you will likely find different benefit segments, as we show in Exhibit 3.8. In this example case, an analysis of the market shows that there are four benefits that customers in the market care about (Benefits 1 through 4). Your goal is to have customers indicate how important each benefit is. For the purpose of the example, assume there are two segments, one that finds Benefits 1 and 2 to be most important and another that finds Benefits 3 and 4 most important.

With benefit segmentation, segments are distinct because customers in different segments care about different benefits or care about them to different degrees. We also see that there are members of each vertical in each segment. So, it's not the verticals that make the segments distinct but rather what set of benefits that customers in each segment care about. Assume as well that we find that Segment 1 is mostly, but not exclusively, in the first vertical (health care plans) and that Segment 2 tends to have more doctors and medical practices. Even in this case, the verticals *are not the bases for segmentation*. Instead, they *describe who is in each segment*. So, you can still market to health care plans and to medical practices/doctors. But now you know how you can deliver more targeted messages—by understanding what benefits they want.

Most important, you will also know which benefits each segment finds most meaningful. Finally, you can see where competitors are focusing their efforts. Since your competitors are most likely oblivious to benefit segmentation, you will gain a strategic advantage.

You can make your life easier by focusing directly on what customers want—i.e., the benefits that they seek. When you segment on benefits, you have a better idea of what benefits different groups of customers want and how important they find these benefits. This is true in all types of markets.

EXHIBIT 3.8. Segmentation on Benefits (Versus Verticals)

Segment	#1	#2
What benefits do they care about	Benefit 1, Benefit 2	Benefit 3, Benefit 4
Are the segments distinct in what they care about?	Yes	Yes
Health care plans	Health care plans in Segment 1	Health care plans in Segment 2
Medical practices/doctors	Medical practices/doctors in Segment 1	Medical practices/doctors in Segment 2

BENEFIT SEGMENTION AND SEGMENT DESCRIPTORS

Does this mean that all the other approaches described in Exhibits 3.2 through 3.5 are irrelevant? Not at all. Although we don't advocate those approaches as ways of segmenting a market, we can use these other ways to *describe* the customers in each benefit segment. For example, if marketers discover that customers want the benefit of status, they can use geographics as a descriptor to indicate where these customers live (urban areas). They can use demographics to show the characteristics of customers in each segment (educated, high income). Finally, marketers can use psychographics to reveal what customers in each segment do in their spare time (i.e., play tennis), what their cultural attitudes and values are (i.e., optimism), and which media they use (*Vogue, Travel + Leisure*). So, you can use benefit segmentation and descriptors together. The former indicates *what people want* and regard as most important. The latter indicates *how to reach them*.

Here is one more example of the difference between benefits and descriptors. Go into the cereal aisle of your grocery store. There is a segment of the cereal market that wants the benefit of sweetness. If you look at this segment, you will see there is a descriptor of age. Specifically, many kids like sweet cereals. However, it's not just kids who want sweet cereal. Trix's commercial showing its crazy rabbit claiming, "Trix, it's not just for kids" embodied the benefit that the brand was relevant to not just little people, but big ones too. So, age (kids, adults) is a descriptor of the segment that cares a lot about sweetness in their cereal. This example also reveals something about descriptors. Sometimes you need to look at brand benefits as a way of entering markets you have not considered. Cereal companies understand this, which is why they offer sweet cereals for kids (e.g., Trix, Count Chocula) and adults too (e.g., Frosted Mini-Wheats).

Use benefit segmentation and descriptors together. The former indicates what people want *and regard as most important. The latter indicates* how to reach them.

So, let's *segment the market using benefits* and think about the classifications (demographics, geographics, verticals, etc.) as *descriptors,* or ways to understand how to reach customers in each segment.

IDENTIFYING BENEFITS SEGMENTS

One thing we've learned is that if you spend time focusing on the process of segmenting the market on benefits and are willing to do the work necessary to determine the benefits that customers want, you will be rewarded with an excellent view of your market. But how do you segment your markets by benefits? First, identify the benefits of your market, using techniques like laddering, explained in appendix A. To make sure the benefits are clearly identified, define each benefit so that the people in your organization who work with customers and segmenting the market are on the same page about what the benefit means. In our experience, not clearly defining benefits leads to disagreements among the people responsible for the brand. Defining benefits clearly helps not only when you are segmenting the market but also later, when you are thinking of ways to increase customers' perceptions of those benefits.

If you spend time focusing on the process of segmenting the market on benefits and are willing to do the work necessary to determine the benefits that customers want, you will be rewarded with an excellent view of your market.

With the benefits clearly defined, the next step is to break up the market into segments. There are several ways to do this: (1) use data, (2) use focus groups, (3) use managerial judgment, and (4) use a combination of data and judgment. First, let's look at how to segment the market empirically using data.

The Data Route

If you are going the data route, identify a random sample of customers in the market and ask how important each benefit is to them. To get information on the relative importance of benefits and how customers trade them off, take all the benefits that have been identified and ask customers to allocate 100 points to those that are most important to them, as we described in chapter two. The more points they allocate to a particular benefit, the more important that benefit is to them. This "constant sum" approach is appropriate with ten or fewer benefits, which is likely the case with most markets.[8] Alternatively, you can use conjoint analysis, a market-research approach that seeks to identify the most influential benefits on respondent choice or decision-making. But be careful when you read about conjoint analysis, since many books illustrate the process using features and attributes rather than benefits.[9]

Before we show you the steps to segment a market using data, let's consider the question of determining the number of segments in a market. The number of segments is a function of three factors: statistical fit (what the empirical data say), what makes the most sense from a managerial point of view, and whether the identified segments can be readily targeted. In our experience, markets tend to have anywhere from three to six distinct segments. So, the challenge (or art) is to find the smallest number of segments that meaningfully differentiate what customers want and find important.

Let's illustrate benefit segmentation using the data approach. Using data is much easier in B2C markets than in B2B markets, since there are many companies that provide consumer panel data. Among them are Amazon's MTurk, Protege Research, Qualtrics, Dynata, and others.

For this example, we looked at the home exercise equipment market using the same set of benefits and price that we examined in chapter two (we provide this data purely for illustrative purposes). We collected data from a panel of five hundred respondents and used the home exercise market as our context. Our sample was composed of people who exercised at least three times per week. We had the respondents allocate 100 points to the various benefits listed, with the number of points indicating how important each benefit was to them. We then used a data analysis technique called cluster analysis to see how the benefits broke out in terms of clusters (or segments).

The analysis began with a "scree plot," which is simply a curve that slopes downward from left to right. The "elbow," at which the curve suddenly changes slope or bends, indicates how many segments there are in the data. Now, determining this point is a judgment call, since it's not always clear when the slope changes, and, in fact, sometimes there is no elbow in the data. The scree plot in our data changed slope at around three or four segments. So, we went with a three-segment solution. The resulting segments are as follows:

Segment 1: Cares mostly about enjoyable and entertaining experiences
Segment 2: Cares mostly about convenience
Segment 3: Cares mostly about the exercise equipment being visually pleasing, the ability to share data, and the ability to signal one's status to others.

Interestingly, most of the home exercise equipment brands that we examined (Peloton, Lululemon Studio Mirror, and Nordic Track) don't seem to directly promote these benefits to consumers. For example, at the time we were writing this book, Peloton's most recent ad campaign was focused on "Motivation That Moves You."[10] Their campaign can certainly tap into the benefit of status identity (Segment 3) but it says little about what that that segment also cares about (the ability to share data and that the exercise equipment is visually pleasing) or what the other segments care mostly about.

When we do benefit segmentation using data, it's very important to also get data about the people who are completing the survey. This data helps you understand which descriptors (e.g., demographics, psychographics, geography, behaviors) are most strongly related to specific segments. The most popular way to do this statistically is through a statistical approach called discriminant analysis.[11] This technique allows you to see whether certain characteristics (income, cohort, interests, etc.) are more strongly associated with one segment than another.

For the purposes of our example, we asked people just a few questions, including their age, gender, and income. In our data, only age was related to segment membership. Segment 1 (enjoyment and entertainment), for example, tended to be composed of older consumers (aged fifty to seventy-five) and negatively related to the youngest age group (eighteen to thirty-five). Segment 2 (convenience) was negatively related to the older age group, meaning the older age group was less likely to be in the segment that cared about convenience. Unfortunately, we have no significant results for Segment 3 (the exercise equipment is visually pleasing, allows users to share data with others, and helps users signal their status), most likely because we collected data on a limited number of descriptors. Asking more questions would likely have resulted in a richer characterization of who is in each segment.

You might wonder how to segment with benefits when you work in an environment where big data is prominent. In appendix D, we talk about big data and getting customer insights, and we suggest ways you might work with customer insight teams to consider benefits in their efforts to get customers' insights, as we discuss in this book.

The Focus Group Route

If you don't have the funds for panel data or the data analysis skills necessary to segment the market empirically, or if you work in a B2B market without access to data, all is not lost. Another way to segment the market is by using focus groups.[12] Here, the organization recruits (or has a research company recruit) groups of consumers or B2B customers (typically between eight and twelve individuals) who buy or are considering a brand from the market.

A trained moderator asks focus group members a predetermined set of questions, with the goal of eventually focusing on the benefits that the focus group members find important. Making sure that everyone has a chance to participate in the discussion ensures that no one person biases the results. Disagreements among focus group members on what benefits are most important to them indicate that there are multiple segments in the market. While focus groups use smaller sample sizes, what you get in return is the ability to ask specific questions about benefits. (For example: What are the benefits? Do some customers in your focus group care about different benefits than others do?)

The Managerial Judgment Route

A third approach is to use the judgment of people responsible for marketing and selling the product (assuming they know what's important to their customers). We have worked with many companies over the years using this approach, and we've learned it requires a shared understanding among people who interface with customers (salespeople, help-desk operators, etc.) as well as more senior people in an organization. The key is to be unbiased and objective. Using managerial judgment requires guidance from someone who can work with the internal team to help them see the bigger picture of the market. In chapter seven, we'll present a case study that uses this approach along with data collected from customers.

The point here is that when you look at the market through the lens of benefits, you can see why it is inefficient to market either with no segmentation or with one of the segmentation approaches we talked about earlier (see Exhibits 3.2–3.5). If you were in the home exercise market, you would know to advertise different benefits to different types of customers. If you just advertise to everybody about how great your status identity is, this will not resonate with the two segments of the market that don't really care a lot about that benefit.

Have You Segmented the Market Correctly?

One question arises often: How do know if you've segmented the market correctly? In our experience, you'll know if you have segmented the market correctly and identified relevant descriptors when the segments are (1) identifiable—in other words, you'll recognize the various segments—(2) measurable, meaning you'll be able to get a size on the segment; (3) differentiated, so that customers in the same segment find the same benefits as important and those in a different segment regard other benefits as important; and (4) reachable from a communications perspective, because you have descriptors that help you reach the target segment. In fact, when we work with companies on benefit segmentation, we've often seen people land on a segmentation of the market that everybody recognizes immediately.

> *When we work with companies on benefit segmentation, we've often seen people land on a segmentation of the market that everybody recognizes immediately.*

Can Customers Jump from One Segment to Another?

In many B2B markets, customers tend to stay in the same segment when making purchasing decisions. This is because their purchasing context doesn't change. However, in consumer markets, customers can sometimes move between segments depending on what situation they are in. Take, for example, going out for dinner. As a consumer yourself, you may go out to dinner at the same restaurant or group of restaurants that offer the same benefits. But on a special occasion, you may go to a completely different restaurant that offers different benefits. So, the situation guides which segment the customer is in. Though the segments don't change, customers can move between segments.

A FEW CAVEATS

Our experience working with companies on benefit segmentation reveals some situations in which you need to be careful when identifying a list of benefits. Here are a few such cases.

Benefits as Potential "Table Stakes"

In some markets, certain benefits may be "table stakes." Table stakes are benefits that all companies provide to the same degree. For example, lightfastness is a necessary benefit of paint—otherwise, the color would immediately fade when exposed to light. But before concluding that some benefit is a table stake, think not just about *whether* all the brands in the market provide the benefit (or not). Think instead about the *level at which* you offer this benefit relative to competitors. For example, one might assume that all cars these days are designed to be safe, but some vehicles are designed to be safer than others, and some customers (i.e., new parents) value that benefit more than others do.

Benefits Wanted by the Entire Market

In some situations, one or more benefits can be important to the entire market. If this is the case, those benefits don't play a role in the segmentation results. If you go back to our data analysis for the home exercise market, and look at the final segments, you'll notice that price is completely missing. You might conclude that people in the market don't care about price when thinking about home exercise equipment. But in this case, as it turns out, almost all the respondents felt that price was most important. It ranked highest in importance of all benefits, with the smallest variance. Essentially everyone wants a low price no matter what segment they are in, and thus this factor played no role in the segmentation. Essentially, all customers use price to screen brands (i.e., "If it's not affordable, I won't consider it") before they make judgements about the brands on the benefits.

Merging Benefits

In some markets, two benefits that were once distinct in customers' minds merge into one. For example, let's say you sell software-as-a-service products related to customer support. Two distinct benefits that your customers may want from such a service are performance (how quickly and easily customers can file a support request) and speed of support (how quickly your service responds to support requests). Imagine that your customers are growing fast and are getting many requests for customer support such that all customers need both performance and speed of support. In this case, the benefits of performance and speed of support may blend into one benefit, called performance.

PLAYBOOK RULE #3

Customers in the market differ in which benefits are most important to them. Segment your market on benefits. Use descriptors like demographics, psychographics, verticals, etc. to characterize who is in each segment.

Segmenting your market by benefits is a powerful tool. The main action point for you, the reader, is to segment your market on benefits using the data, focus group, or managerial judgment routes described earlier in the chapter and to determine which descriptors are most strongly associated with each benefit segment. Before moving on, let's summarize the main points.

KEY TAKEAWAYS

1. Segmenting your market by benefits allows you to focus on what customers want.
2. Take all the other ways people talk about segmenting and see which are the best descriptors of customers in each segment. These other ways do not give you a strategic view of the market

as a whole and the competitive landscape, but they can provide helpful information about who is in each segment and how to reach them.

3. There are various approaches to segmenting your market on benefits (data, focus group, managerial judgment routes). Make sure to follow the guidelines that explain how you know you've segmented the market correctly.
4. Segmenting the market on benefits requires far less data than AI or machine learning does. If you want to get insights, use benefits as the basis of segmenting your market. In appendix D, we explain how this might be done.

As we will see in chapter four, the segments you have identified and the perceptual map you have developed in chapter two form the basis for targeting and positioning decisions; these are the topics we discuss next.

TARGET AND POSITION ON BENEFITS

By now, you realize that focusing on customer benefits will reward you with the greatest marketing impact. Because customers buy brands that offer the benefits they seek, any other way of doing marketing results in wasted resources. So far, however, we haven't fully linked benefits to marketing actions. In this chapter, we begin to shift emphasis as we move from market segmentation to targeting and positioning.

STP VERSUS TP

Some readers might have heard the marketing acronym STP, which stands for segmenting (which we discussed in chapter three), targeting, and positioning (ideas that we discuss in this chapter). Segmentation, targeting, and positioning are critical strategic decisions, because the results of these decisions guide all marketing efforts. After organizations have gone through these strategic decisions, they can better assess the human and monetary resources needed to make their brand a success in the marketplace.

As we mentioned in chapter three, most organizations don't segment their market on benefits. Instead, they focus on some demographic, vertical, or other group, or fail to segment the market at all. In short, they don't do the segmentation part of this process—instead reducing it to TP! Organizations often ignore segmentation and instead target some demographic or vertical and then go right to brand positioning—but the position is not based on what customers care about. Now, TP is certainly important . . . but mostly in the bathroom, not in the boardroom. By ignoring segmentation, targeting and positioning become less thoughtful—and less effective—processes.

TARGET SEGMENT SELECTION

Targeting (or target segment selection) is the process of determining which of the various segments uncovered from the market segmentation exercise in chapter three should be the focus of your organization's marketing efforts. Targeting is critical. Indeed, why would you attempt to target all customers in the market with your brand if your market segmentation showed you that not all customers want the same benefits? Additionally, targeting all customers in the market can be an inefficient use of both time and money.

Some people might think that targeting is restricting because it forces you to focus on one segment. We show that targeting is not restricting at all—in fact, you have a great deal of flexibility when choosing target segments. You can even target more than one segment. In fact, many everyday consumer products target all segments in their markets, though they do so with different brands and different brand positioning statements.

TARGETING OPTIONS

So, let's begin with a focus on targeting. In the last chapter we provided an illustration of segmenting the home exercise market. Recall that we found three segments. Let's continue to use that three-segment market to illustrate the process of targeting, here using a different example. Remember, not all markets are composed of just three segments, so this is purely an illustration. In Exhibit 4.1 is a graphical representation of three segments, which we'll call S_1, S_2, and S_3.

EXHIBIT 4.1. Market Segmentation Indicates Three Segments

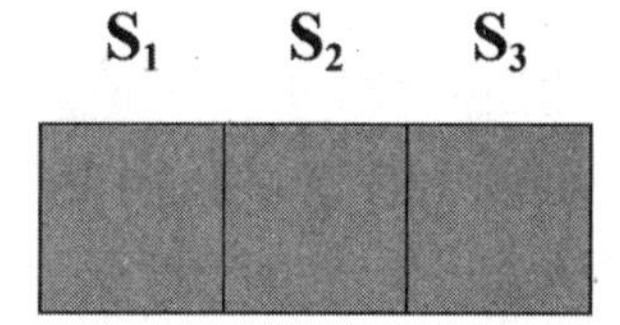

Targeting Multiple Segments

Again, targeting doesn't necessarily mean you cannot go after more than one segment—it's just that you need to do so in a strategic and defensible manner. For example, the computer chip market (which we will discuss further in the case study in chapter seven) comprises three distinct segments, as in Exhibit 4.1. We named the three segments

"Innovators," "Pragmatists," and "Quick & Easy." The Innovators were primarily interested in the benefit of high performance. The Pragmatists wanted a balance of performance for a reasonable price, and Quick & Easy mainly wanted the benefits of ease of use and technical support.

Targeting doesn't necessarily mean you cannot go after more than one segment—it's just that you need to do so in a strategic and defensible manner.

Based on the results of a benefit segmentation exercise, the company decided to target one of these segments immediately, given its growth rate and the competitive environment. The plan was to target a second segment after the company had built up the organizational strengths needed to enter that segment with the same brand. The third segment would be targeted even later. Essentially, the company would go after the entire market (all three segments) over time. We call this a target segment migration strategy.

Targeting Subsegments

You don't necessarily need to target the entire benefit segment. Instead, you can target one or more descriptors associated with a benefit segment. Recall from chapter three that when identifying benefit segments, we also identified descriptors that indicate who the customers in each segment are. Such information helps you to understand how to reach customers in that segment (their demographics, verticals, lifestyles, etc.). Hence, when marketing efforts focus on who to target, we already know quite a bit about the benefits that those customers want and who they are.

It is possible that an organization can use various descriptors to identify subsegments. Given our three-segment market and the decision to target customers who want a specific set of benefits, represented by S_1, we might target only some of the customers in Segment 1, based on certain descriptors, as Exhibit 4.2 shows. For example, let's say you sell deodorants, and you target segment S_1, which cares mostly about the experiential benefit of being unscented. The descriptors associated with this market include adult women, adult men, and kids. Your organization might decide to target this segment, but target only the adult men and adult women, rather than the entire segment, which also includes kids. In this case, you are targeting two subsegments of the benefit segment S_1. Targeting subsegments might make sense, if, for example, your marketing resources are stretched. It might also make sense to focus on those subsegments who are easiest to reach or who already buy the brand you sell (i.e., users versus non-users or buyers versus non-buyers). The same is true in B2B markets, where we might focus on only a subset of customers in the segment, such as those in a particular vertical or those in a particular geographic area.

EXHIBIT 4.2. Targeting One Benefit Segment and Two Subsegments

	S_1	S_2	S_3
Adult Women	(shaded)		
Adult Men	(shaded)		
Kids			

Let's generalize the possibilities with the following example, in which there are three descriptors, labeled D_1, D_2, and D_3. You can target one segment and one descriptor, as in Exhibit 4.3, for example. The company Keep It Kind does this, targeting one segment in the deodorant market (kids who want unscented deodorant). Their product, called Fresh Kidz, is a deodorant that emphasizes the benefits of safety and health (which we will label as segment S_2) targeted at the kids subsegment (D_3).

EXHIBIT 4.3. Targeting One Benefit Segment and One Subsegment

	S_1	S_2	S_3
D_1			
D_2			
D_3		■	

At the other extreme, some organizations cover the entire market by targeting all segments and all descriptors, as in Exhibit 4.4, using different brands.

Procter & Gamble (P&G) understands this benefit approach well. Different Tide brands appeal to different benefits that customers expect from their laundry detergent. For example, there is Tide Brights + Whites Rescue for customers wanting the benefit of brighter colors and whites in their clothes. If you need the benefit of deep cleaning, they have Hygienic Clean, or Tide PODS for the benefit of odor removal. Most other benefits that customers want (e.g., stain

EXHIBIT 4.4. Targeting All Benefit Segments and Across All Descriptors

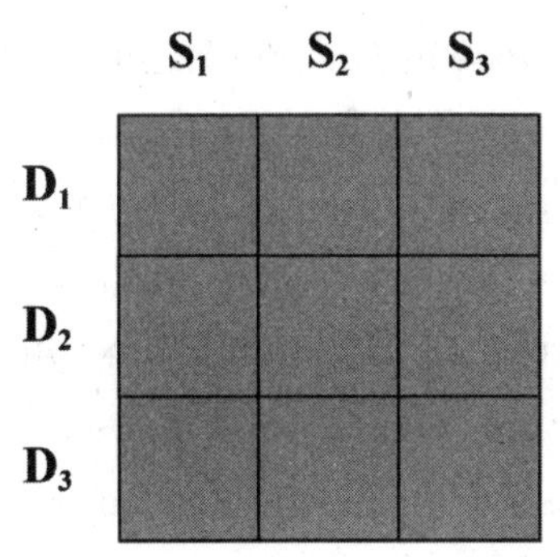

removal, friendliness to sensitive skin) are the focus of various other Tide products.

You have a great deal of flexibility in which benefit segments (or subsegments) to target. Think about these possibilities as you make your targeting decision. And remember, this is not a static decision; you can target one segment now and another segment later.

Targeting in the Property and Casualty Insurance Industry

In 2017, Liberty Mutual was a significant player in the auto and home insurance business. "The insurance category is a competitive space, and there is a need to break through to capture people's attention," said Jeff Goodby, co-chairman and partner at Goodby, Silverstein & Partners, a full-service advertising agency based in San Francisco. He provided creative content for the 2019 "LiMu Emu and Doug" campaign, which is still running as we write this book.[1] The main tagline of the campaign is the phrase "Only Pay for What You Need." While this phrase received a lot of good and bad press, the campaign overall was well-targeted toward a segment that cares about two benefits—affordability and the ability to customize insurance options.

Customization is a benefit that shows up in many markets and brands (for example, customize the music you want on Spotify; customize your running shoes with Nike). However, as lawyer H. Dennis Beaver writes, "The truth is that all insurance companies allow the customer to customize their policy."[2] Of course, this may be true, but all the other companies are targeting different segments. State Farm is currently promoting itself with the tagline "Surprisingly Great Rates," presumably catering to a segment that cares most about low price. But if you live in a high fire zone, as we do, you may be in a different segment of home insurance market, and favor benefits like major hazard protection.

CRITERIA FOR CHOOSING THE RIGHT TARGET SEGMENT(S)

In general, organizations target those benefit segments that offer the greatest potential for their brand. A set of criteria identified here can be helpful in assessing such potential.

Once you have segmented the market on benefits, you can then examine the *size* of each segment. Larger segments may have more potential, assuming that your brand has the benefits customers in a large segment find important. It's possible to estimate segment size using the data gathered when segmenting the market. If you can determine the size of the market as a whole (say, using industry reports or data published from trade associations), and if you know the percentage of customers from your benefit segmentation exercise that are associated with each of the segments, you could estimate the size of each segment. For example, if you operate in a $100M market and 40 percent of sampled customers fell into Segment 1, the size of the segment would be $40M. You could use the same process for any descriptor that plays a role in characterizing who is in the segment.

When segments differ in terms of the benefits they want and how they use the brand, this can be useful for estimating segment size too. For example, imagine that you sell computer chips to business customers. One segment uses the chips uniquely to produce gaming console machines. Estimating the size of the video game machine market is relatively easy (in terms of sales). Statista predicts $217.06 billion in 2022, but data on console unit sales is available as well.[3] Finally, if you find that certain age groups or other demographics describe your segment, the size can be derived directly from the size of the age group or other demographic.

Growing segments also have more potential than do segments that are stagnant or declining in growth. Segment *growth rate* can be assessed by observing recent and anticipated changes in the size of the segment. There are many industry reports from companies like Statista and Mintel that provide an overview of growth rates that you can apply to understanding the growth of the segments.

Before entering a new segment, you should also consider the *development costs* associated with entering a segment and any *synergies* that might occur by entering and gaining expertise in that segment. To a certain extent, these criteria are a function of how *reachable* the segment is. If it is clearer how to reach one segment based on its descriptors than it is a second one, it will be less costly and more efficient to target that first segment.

So, to determine which benefit segment to target, ask yourself:

- How big is this benefit segment?
- Is it growing?
- What are the marketing costs of entering this benefit segment? Are customers in this segment reachable?
- Does targeting this benefit segment create any synergies for us now or in the future?

Based on the answers to these questions, you will be able to see the segments you should target clearly.

Some readers might think these steps are meant for only large marketing teams. But even a single person can gather this information and answer these questions. Remember, when you have a large marketing team, you need to get consensus to move forward with consistency. If you are a marketing team of one, you don't have this problem.

Finally, some of the companies we have worked with experience the targeting decision as something that literally touches on the soul of the company. That is because it takes discipline and a willingness to let go of focusing on the entire market. As you'll see in later chapters, it requires a deep look at the company and its capabilities as well as the competitive landscape. Nonetheless, our clients have always found it easy to decide which segment(s) to target and what segment(s) to leave behind.

BRAND POSITIONING

Once you decide which segment to target, the next step is to position your brand to customers in that benefit segment.

What Brand Positioning IS

We define **brand positioning** as a process of determining how you want customers in your target segment to perceive the benefits of your brand relative to competitors' brands. In other words, with positioning you determine what image you want customers to have of your brand, including what makes it different from your competitors' brands. When marketers position a brand, they develop a promise to customers about what distinct set of benefits customers will receive from buying and using their brand.

For example, Southwest Airlines positioned its brand as different from competitors by being a no-frills airline that nonetheless gave customers a superior in-flight experience by virtue of its fun, casual, and highly service-oriented flight attendants. Southwest also offered more traveler-friendly policies relative to competing brands.[4] To use another example, Amazon positions itself as the largest consumer and business-to-business retailer in the US, and it offers an incredible assortment of products at competitive prices, shipped for free (for Prime members), arriving at one's home or place of business within a few days, and with the option of free returns.

Sometimes, existing brands need to be repositioned—or associated with a different set of benefits than before. For example, at one point in its history, Old Spice deodorant was viewed by younger men as something for old men. To regain its relevance, Old Spice repositioned the brand around the theme of freshness through its Fresh Collection products.[5] Additionally, Philips, the Dutch maker of such products as Sonicare electric toothbrushes, Norelco shavers, and home lighting and audio equipment, was facing tight competition from Japanese manufacturers in the US market. Customers didn't see what made Philips's brands special. In response, Philips worked to reposition its brands as having superior technology that is convenient and easy to use. Similarly, in early 2010s, PAM lost its leadership position over the cooking spray market to less expensive store brands. Because customers saw little difference between PAM and store-brand cooking sprays, they bought PAM only when it was on sale. Moreover, some consumers avoided PAM altogether, worrying that cooking sprays would change the taste of food. To rectify these brand challenges, PAM introduced a new and improved formula and utilized proof points that demonstrated the nonstick superiority of PAM compared with store brands.[6]

What Brand Positioning IS NOT

For some reason, positioning is a deeply misunderstood concept, and so we want to be equally clear about what positioning is and what it is not. Positioning is not simply selling your brand in a new product category, since a brand in a new category still needs to be positioned. Positioning is not messaging. Positioning is a process; messaging is the communication efforts that follow from that process. Nor is positioning a brand name, though sometimes a brand's name can help to make its benefits clear. For example, the brand name "Affresh" washing machine cleaner clearly communicates the benefit of making the inside of your washing machine smell fresh.

Why Not Position on Features?

Perhaps, like many organizations, you're thinking about positioning your brand in terms of its features (e.g., a backlit magic keyboard) rather than its benefits (clear visibility). There is, of course a relationship between features and benefits, since features give rise to benefits, as we showed in Exhibit 1.1. But the problem with positioning on features is that you are asking customers to *translate* the features into benefits. Experts in your product category might be able to do this quite readily. For example, computer experts know what a 3.2GHz Intel Xeon W processor with Turbo Boost up to 4.2GHz and a 19MB cache can do for them. However, information regarding these features would leave nonexperts flummoxed about what these features will do for them and why they are important. The second problem is that features are *all about you* and your organization rather than about *customers* and what they want. As such, positioning on features can cause brands to lack relevance to targeted customers.

The problem with positioning on features is that you are asking customers to* translate *the features into benefits.

Many technology companies focus on features. We have seen several technology consultants who call this an "inside-out" approach to positioning or creating a desired image for a company and its products. This approach is all about what the organization wants, rather than what the customers want—in short, it's backward. For example, Samsung is currently running a TV spot for their Galaxy Z Flip4 phone, centered on the feature of a flip phone. When the focus is on features, the main tagline will derive from the feature. The Galaxy Z Flip4 tagline is "Unfold Your World." Perhaps this is a benefit—but does anybody really want to unfold their world? And if they did, would a flip cell phone really do the trick? It's not that features aren't important . . . they are. They can give rise to benefits. But the focus of positioning should be on benefits.

Positioning and Perceptual Maps

Recall the discussion in chapter two about the need to think in terms of both the customer and the organizational sides of the market when positioning your brand. Remember, how *you want customers to perceive your brand* is not the same as how those customers *actually view* your brand. In chapter two, we discussed how customers have associations linked to a brand, among which are the brand's benefits. Positioning is successful when the benefits that the organization *wants* customers to associate with its brand are the same as the benefits that customers *do* associate with the brand. In this case, the desired benefit perceptions and the actual benefit perceptions are the same (i.e., aligned).

Positioning is successful when the benefits that the organization wants customers to associate with its brand are the same as the benefits that customers do associate with the brand.

A perceptual map can prove highly useful when thinking about how to position your brand. Recall from chapter two that a perceptual map depicts how customers perceive the benefits of various brands in the market. *Perceptual maps are all about customers* and their images of brands on the market. *Positioning is all about the organization*, and the image they want customers to have of their brand in terms of its benefits.

It is possible that when thinking about how to position (or reposition) a brand that there may be a *gap* between the way customers perceive the brand and how you want them to see it based on your proposed positioning. You can represent this gap on the perceptual map, showing how customers currently perceive of your brand and how you want them to perceive it after you have executed on your positioning.

The effectiveness of your marketing can be revealed by how much you have closed this gap.

Positioning Choices

When it comes to positioning, organizations have a choice of whether to (a) position their brand as close to competitors, such as the market leader; (b) position their brand as better than current competitors; or (c) position their brand as different from competitors.

Let's address these options one by one. Why would an organization choose to position their brand as being close to a competitor on the same benefits? Doing so makes sense when markets are growing, there is a leading competitor in the segment, and your brand is new. By positioning one's brand as similar to a leading brand, customers are likely to infer that the new brand has similar benefits to the leader. Additionally, because the market leader is a well-known brand, customers may remember the new brand better given its presumed proximity to a leading competitive brand. One challenge is that this strategy may not be sustainable, since it may be difficult to attract market share away from the leader over the long term, particularly if the market stops growing and competition becomes more and more fierce.

An alternative is to position your brand as better than competitors. San Francisco–based clothing brand Everlane appeals to consumers who might have purchased clothing from retailers like J.Crew, which, like Everlane, sells clothing basics. However, Everlane touts an added benefit: sustainable product sourcing. This added benefit gives Everlane a competitive advantage over J.Crew, which has lost market share to Everlane. By adding a benefit that competitors do not offer (such as sustainable sourcing, a benefit the segment wants) or by providing a higher level of the benefit than what competitors offer, the brand can have a leg up on competitor brands. This strategy makes sense if the brand can authentically and convincingly demonstrate its benefit superiority relative to competitors. Everlane's sustainability benefit is noted extensively on its website under the name of "radical transparency."

A third positioning strategy is to position one's brand as different from competitors. Bang energy drink claims to be different from Red Bull and Monster brands because Bang includes creatine, an ingredient that purportedly builds muscle mass. The drink has been popular with athletes and bodybuilders. Similarly, the dating app The League positions itself away from other dating apps like eHarmony by emphasizing its focus on career-minded people looking for long-term relationships. It also offers users the opportunity to go on three online dates over the course of a nine-minute video chat. Users can also upload videos of themselves so that dating prospects can see what they really look and sound like, not just what they look like in pictures.

POSITIONING STATEMENTS

So far, we've emphasized the importance of identifying benefits in a market (chapter one), developing a perceptual map of brands in the market (chapter two), segmenting the market (chapter three), and engaging in targeting and positioning (this chapter, so far). What we haven't gotten to yet is pulling all the ideas in these plays together (along with some ideas in chapters five and six) to develop a positioning statement.

What Is a Positioning Statement?

A **positioning statement** is a two- to three-sentence summary that specifies (1) what target segment you want to focus on, (2) the benefits that your brand offers to customers in this target segment, and (3) a set of proof points that specify why you can offer these benefits better than competitors can. Positioning reflects the promise you plan to make to that segment you are targeting, and a positioning statement is a document, internal to the organization, that formally declares that promise. It's the positioning statement that guides all marketing activities. For this reason, it is a critical element of marketing strategy. If you target more than one segment, you will need more positioning statements, since the different segments care about different benefits.

Positioning statements are not pretty. They are not awesome or amazing. Instead, they are the foundation for building pretty and awesome *messaging*. A strong foundation will keep a house from collapsing or getting blown away by a strong wind—as long as the frame (the messaging) is connected to the foundation (the positioning statement). There are many different types of positioning statements available online (though rarely are they focusing on benefits). One common element is that the statement includes an explanation of why your brand differs from your competition.

We advocate that a positioning statement include three core elements. The first two are easy and follow directly from the market segmentation exercise and target segment selection process.

1. The first element is a statement of the segment you are targeting.
2. The second states what benefits customers this segment want. Typically, a segment cares most about two or three benefits.

3. Finally, the third states the proof points that support why your brand can provide the benefits desired by the segment better or differently than competitors. (We say a lot more about these proof points in Plays #5 and #6, where we talk about what makes a positioning statement credible and defensible.)

Here are some examples of positioning statements:[7]

- For local and international travelers [selected target segment], Airbnb is the only booking website that connects you to unique experiences all over the world [benefits] because we offer the largest and most diverse selection of places to stay, which are top-rated and personalized [proof points].
- Dove is the only personal care product that helps everyday women develop a positive relationship with the way you look, because we create products that deliver real results and are trusted by more women than our competitors.
- For patients suffering regularly from acid reflux, Nexium is the only prescription or OTC acid reflux medication that can heal your acid reflux, because it has the most powerful mechanism of action.

Remember, the positioning statement is an internal document that details your promise to customers. In chapter eight, we talk extensively about how to ensure that customers perceive the benefits of your brand in the way you intended.

Misconceptions About Positioning Statements

Unfortunately, there are a lot of misconceptions about what positioning statements are. One common misconception is that a positioning statement is the same as an organization's tagline,[8] while others say it's a combination of customers' needs and price,[9] although they never specify what they mean by "needs," and not every customer segment cares about price.

Some people think a brand positioning statement is a "statement of ambition about the future the brand intends to build. It's a creative activity, fueled by visionary thinking, and can take several 'flavours': a vision; a mission statement."[10] In other words, it is inspirational, creative, and beautiful. Messaging can be inspirational, creative, and beautiful too, but it should build on the foundation laid by the brand's positioning statement.

Positioning Statements and Stress Tests

We've noted that positioning statements are internal documents that guide the entire marketing effort. If done correctly, a positioning statement is a challenge to create, because finalizing one requires stress tests to make sure it's credible and defensible. You will notice from the play titles that the next two chapters (chapters five and six) discuss stress tests.

You may have heard about stress tests in other contexts—like in medicine. A patient is asked to walk or run on a treadmill to see how they perform. The treadmill provides the stress. The goal of the stress test is to make sure the patient is healthy and can take steps to increase their health. The stress tests we discuss in the next few chapters are designed to find evidence that supports the proof points in the positioning statements, thereby making them more credible and defensible. Such evidence comes from looking deeply at your organization (chapter five) and your competitors (chapter six). If such evidence is lacking, you might consider targeting a different segment whose benefits you can more readily provide. For this reason, even if you apply the ideas about targeting and positioning discussed in this chapter perfectly, you should still regard your own targeting and position decisions as preliminary. "Definitive plans" for targeting and positioning will come after the stress tests discussed in the next two chapters are performed. After the stress tests, you can be confident about your final positioning statement.

PLAYBOOK RULE #4

Without having a perceptual map, it is difficult, if not impossible, to position your brand and see if customer perceptions have changed or not.

By now, you'll have a deeper understanding about targeting and positioning. The main action point for you, the reader, at this point is to target a segment in your market on benefits and put together a preliminary positioning statement. Before moving on, let's summarize the main points.

KEY TAKEAWAYS

1. Targeting involves determining which segments you should focus on. You can target more segments via a target segment migration strategy.
2. You can target the entire segment or a subsegment.

3. Positioning statements are a promise to customers. They are not a creative message but are the foundations on which to build creative messages.
4. Once you have a positioning statement that is defensible and credible, focus on the features and attributes that are directly related to the benefits promise to the market segment you targeted.

PASS THE CREDIBILITY STRESS TEST

The positioning statement(s) you constructed in chapter four is a promise to customers in your target segments. Before moving forward with this promise, it's essential to assess whether a positioning statement is credible to the market and will provide you with a long-term differential advantage over your competitors. The following two chapters will subject your promise to two "stress tests." A **stress test** is a test of the resilience of your positioning statement. Through a stress test, you'll find out if you need to change your positioning statement to make it more robust, compelling, and credible. You might even change your target segment based on these stress tests.

CAN YOUR ORGANIZATION PULL IT OFF?

Our use of stress tests echoes a well-known, but rarely followed, saying by the ancient Chinese military strategist Sun Tzu. In *The Art of War*, he points to knowing yourself (i.e., your organization) and the competition as essential to long-term advantage:

> If you *know the enemy* and *know yourself*, you need not fear the result of a hundred battles. If you know yourself but not the enemy, for every victory gained you will also suffer a defeat. If you know neither the enemy nor yourself, you will succumb in every battle.

In this chapter, we'll focus on *knowing ourselves*. We're doing this because we are not positioning a brand in a vacuum; we need to make sure our brand and the organization of which it is a part have the capabilities to fulfill any brand positioning statement we develop. First, you will analyze your organization and assess whether you can deliver on the benefits that customers in the market want. Second, you will try to understand how your proposed positioning for the brand fits within the organization's strengths, core competencies, and brand architecture. Finally, you will analyze other factors associated with your organization that can affect the credibility or success of the proposed positioning. By doing this work, you are not only assuring yourself that your organization can pull off your positioning, but you are also identifying proof points that support the benefits noted in your positioning statement. In the next chapter we help you *know the enemy* (ha! ha!—your competitors) by playing a competitive, dynamic game. By playing this game and looking at other aspects of your competition, you will be more assured that your positioning statement is defensible.

ORGANIZATIONAL STRENGTHS AND BRAND BENEFITS

To carry out a stress test on your positioning statement, you need to know your organization's underlying capabilities or strengths beyond just superficial assessments. Strengths are essential for any organization and its strategic efforts, but for our purposes, *we are interested in strengths that match up with the benefits in our positioning statement* and are hence proof points that credibly support the positioning statement. A benefits-strengths analysis (Exhibit 5.1) can help you systematically match the benefits in the positioning statement with the organization's abilities.

We are interested in strengths that match up with the benefits in our positioning statement *and are hence proof points that credibly support the positioning statement.*

Imagine you are targeting two segments that, together, want four benefits, and you have identified four strengths of your organization. Now examine whether these benefits match up to your organization's strengths. This match between benefits and strengths is presented in Exhibit 5.1 on the next page.

A match between a benefit noted in your positioning statement and a strength of your organization adds a proof point that indicates why you can deliver on this benefit. This proof point adds to the credibility of your positioning statement. In the example in Exhibit 5.1, low manufacturing costs are a strength of the organization, if the brand aims to position itself as having low prices. These two things are matched; the fact that the organization keeps manufacturing costs low means that it can credibly provide low prices. There are also organizational strengths that support the Ease of Use and Service benefits. However, there are

EXHIBIT 5.1. Mapping Benefits to Organizational Strengths

Benefits in the Proposed Positioning Statements	Organizational Strengths			
	Low Manufacturing Costs	Deep Knowledge of Customers	Strong Research and Development	High-Quality Salespeople
Low Prices	X			
Ease of Use		X		
Service		X		X
The Product Is Entertaining to Use				

X: Represents a direct relationship between an organizational strength and a benefit

no organizational strengths that match the benefit of Entertaining to Use. Since the organization does not have strengths in this benefit, it might be appropriate to reevaluate (and perhaps drop) this benefit from the positioning statement.

Although your organization may possess inherent strengths, a comprehensive understanding of your brand's strengths (and weaknesses) can be achieved only by examining its entire value chain. Let's discuss this next.

Your Organization's Value Chain

When you look at your organization, you see people, maybe a building, a parking lot, your office, various meeting rooms, etc. That is the way most people see their organization. But, like looking through a twisting kaleidoscope, there are other ways to look at all organizations, and these other ways go beyond conventional ways of describing what you do. Business strategist and Harvard professor Michael Porter has suggested a new and very popular way to look at organizations that can reveal an organization's strengths and weaknesses: the value chain approach.[1] Essentially, a **value chain** describes an organization's activities in transforming inputs like raw materials and components into finished products and services delivered to customers. For our purposes, the point of this approach is to see if there are any unique strengths (or hidden weaknesses) you might have along this value chain and to assess how these strengths (or weaknesses) might affect the credibility of your positioning statement.

A simplified way of thinking about your value chain focuses on three primary activities: (1) downstream activities (i.e., activities that your organization uses to deliver your brand to customers), (2) upstream activities (i.e., activities your organization relies on as inputs to its business), and (3) internal activities (i.e., what your organization does with the upstream activities to turn them into a finished brand).

Let's assume that you have a product, service, experience, or other type of brand. Depending on your organization, *downstream activities* might include selling to intermediaries, like retailers or fulfillment services, and working with advertising agencies. It also might consist of shipping, installation, and other postpurchase activities. For example, if you are a medical practice, downstream activities might include things like gaining PR or social media for your practice, billing customers, handling insurance claims, and working with services that maintain your physical space. If you are an actor, downstream activities might include working with the networks or movie companies to promote a new movie, participating in talk shows to talk about it, taking activities needed to maintain or build relationship with fans, etc. You can see why these are called "downstream" since they happen after you have made what you are selling.

Of course, to make your brand, you need *upstream activities* too. Upstream activities include inputs from other organizations that are needed to make your brand. So, if you're a nonprofit organization, upstream activities would likely include finding donors and volunteers. If you are a fashion organization, upstream activities might include working with fabric producers and garment fabrication companies (assuming fabrication is done by someone else). If you are an actor, upstream activities include work with an agent, acting coach, and lawyer who can help to procure a role in a movie or show. If you sell coffee in cafés, your upstream activity might be sourcing different coffee beans. If you are an interior design organization, your upstream activities might include your relationships with suppliers and all the activities required to receive, store, and disseminate inputs to the design process. The upstream activities analysis would include the number and capacity of suppliers, the nature of contracts, the quality of materials, and perhaps movement toward digital transformation (e.g., smart manufacturing).

Finally, there are *internal activities* that reflect what your organization actually does itself. If you are a medical practice, internal activities include activities of the physicians and staff, the use of on-site medical equipment, the nature and quality of the exam rooms, and so on. If you are an actor, internal activities include work with a producer, camera crew, director, and other members of the cast. Depending on the brand at hand, these activities might include product/design and manufacturing. Peloton has software design, testing interfaces, user interfaces, and in-house production of its products. In other contexts, the analyses can include how quickly you produce goods and services, investments in capacity, or labor force quality, among other possibilities.

Now, this view of a value chain (upstream, internal, downstream) is simple, but you can make it far more complex if you want. In fact, you may need to if you are in a large, complex, or multibrand organization.[2]

Regardless of how simple or complex your view of the value chain is, examining activities throughout your value chain can help you identify strengths that support (i.e., provide proof points to) the benefits noted in your positioning statement. Let's illustrate these ideas with a few examples and show how they relate to strengths. Walmart's "Everyday Low Price" positioning is credible because they have leveraged strengths in their value chain. Even with competition from Amazon, Walmart is reported to have on average 34 percent lower prices.[3] Their value chain reveals how they get these low prices. For example, they have opted to work with manufacturers directly, cutting out the costs of other intermediaries like traders (wholesalers). Historically, they eliminated storage costs by unloading items from an incoming semitrailer truck or railroad car and loading these materials directly into outbound trucks, trailers, or railcars (and vice versa), with no storage in between.

As another example, IKEA launched a comprehensive sustainability positioning strategy in 2012 called "People & Planet Positive"[4] that focused on the organization's value chain, from how and where they sourced raw materials to life at their customers' homes. They positioned themselves as creating a movement in society about better living, inspiring and enabling people to live healthier, more sustainable lives.

This example shows that your value chain might extend downstream all the way out to your customers' daily lives.

You might also find weaknesses in the value chain that make it more difficult for you to support the benefits in your positioning statement. For example, let's say you run an online store that sells jewelry, which you import from a single source in China. Your brand benefits include beautiful and high-quality jewels that are in ready supply. However, because you work with a single source, you are dependent on them. For example, if they fold or if you place a large order that they can't handle, you and your brand's growth potential and your ability to deliver on your benefits will be negatively affected. So, this is a weakness in the upstream part of the value chain. Such a dependency is common when examining a value chain, as Ford recently found out when the delivery of certain vehicles was delayed because the production line didn't have enough of the brand-consistent blue oval badges that mark cars as Fords.[5]

> ***Examining activities throughout your value chain can help you identify strengths that support (i.e., provide proof points to) the benefits noted in your positioning statement.***

Benefits and Value Chain Strengths

For your positioning statement to be credible, it should also take into account whether your benefits are supported (or not) by your value chain. *This requires a value chain analysis.*

To start a value chain analysis, take the benefits from your positioning statement and revisit the perceptual map for your brand. If, for example, you are perceived as close to a competitor in a segment that you targeted, then look at your value chain and see if you can credibly differentiate by convincing customers to perceive you as much better than competitors on the benefits desired by that segment. By placing your attention on the benefits desired, you can examine which parts of the value chain can be enhanced to provide more of those benefits.

For example, if you and your competitor are trying to appeal to a segment that wants reliability, is there a way to create a brand with higher-quality components (upstream activities), design, and operations (product design/manufacturing activities) with more reliability? If a segment wants lower prices, is there a way to reduce expenses throughout the value chain? Can you leverage experience curve effects (the decline in cost per unit that comes with increase in number of units and experience)? These experience curve effects could allow for aggressive pricing against competitors. If a segment wants a symbolic benefit, like status, where in your value chain can you find ways to provide this benefit? By focusing on product design, Apple's operations and marketing team was able to break out of a commodity cell phone market with symbolic benefits like "coolness" and experiential benefits like touch screens. It even developed unique packaging, which became standard for many organizations' packaging today.

In short, organizations can focus on activities in the value chain that can help them credibly deliver on the benefits noted in the positioning statement.

The Power of Core Competencies

Because you are focusing on strengths that directly support benefits, its useful to stop and consider an important type of organizational strength–brand benefit relationship: a core competency.[6] **Core competencies** are broadly defined as key capabilities that reflect what your organization does *uniquely well*. Core competencies are important to an organization because they can help an organization distinguish its brands from its competitors and reduce costs more than competitors do, thereby attaining a competitive advantage. Your positioning statement is highly credible when the benefits in the positioning statement are core competencies.

There are three tests to identify core competencies. The first test involves matching your strengths to benefits. Your strengths must make "a significant contribution to the perceived customer benefits of the end product."[7] So, in a table like Exhibit 5.1, there must be at least one X, and ideally strengths along the value chain as well. In addition, the strength supporting the benefit cannot be temporary, such as strength built on a patent that will expire soon; it must be a strength that is relatively enduring over time. A second test of a core competency is that the strengths cannot be easily imitated by competitors. If competitors can readily copy your strengths, the competency will not be an enduring one. A third test is that these strengths, and the benefits they are associated with, allow or have allowed you to compete in other markets. Such strengths also tend to cross internal organizational boundaries.

If you have strengths with these qualities, they are core competencies for your organization. And if these core competencies support the benefits in your positioning statement, your statement will be more credible. These strengths will also assist you in in developing paths for growth—a topic we discuss in chapter eight.

BRAND BENEFITS AND BRAND ARCHITECTURE

Another factor associated with your organization that can affect the credibility of your brand's positioning statement is the brand architecture that your company uses. **Brand architecture** refers to how the various brands that make up the organization (or parent brand) are related. If your organization has only one brand, this part of the chapter will not be relevant to you. For everyone else, read on.

Consider the set of brands associated with the FedEx Corporation parent brand. FedEx offers a broad portfolio of transportation, e-commerce, and business service solutions within its brand portfolio, all of which include the FedEx name. Some people call this type of branding structure a "branded house" because all brands in the FedEx portfolio share the FedEx name. If FedEx were to introduce a new brand, chances are it would include the FedEx name too. Originally, FedEx was just a package delivery organization. However, as the organization grew, it extended the original FedEx name to include other services besides package delivery, including services like FedEx Office and FedEx Freight.

Compare the FedEx brand architecture with that of Procter & Gamble. P&G offers different brands of diapers (e.g., All Good, Charlie Banana, Luvs, and Pampers), brands of fabric care (e.g., Ariel, Bounce, Cheer, Downy, Dreft, Era, Gain, and Tide), different paper care brands (Bounty, Charmin, Puffs), and different brands of grooming products (Braun, Gillette, Joy + Glee, Venus, the Art of Shaving). All categories in which P&G offers products (which include those mentioned here as well as hair care, feminine care, home care, oral care, personal health care, and skin and personal care) have different brand names. P&G's brand architecture is described as a "house of brands," meaning that within the P&G corporation, each brand has its own unique or independent brand name. If P&G introduced a new brand, chances are it would have an independent brand name too.

If your organization uses a "branded house," like FedEx, presumably the brands that compose the organization share benefits in common. With FedEx, the brand stands for the benefits of efficient service operations and high-quality solutions to customers' and businesses' problems. If FedEx offers a new brand, its benefits would ideally align with the benefits of the other brands in the FedEx brand portfolio. To the extent that it does, the "speedy delivery" and "high-quality business solutions" benefits in a positioning statement would be highly credible, since that's what all brands in the brand portfolio stand for. If the new brand has a positioning statement that states different benefits (e.g., the hypothetical FedEx Landscaping, with benefits like superior irrigation systems and flexibility in garden services), the credibility of the positioning statement would be compromised, since the identity of the brand and that of the organization are not aligned. In short, if you are a branded house organization with a family of brands, the benefits in your positioning statement should align with what the organizational brand stands for. If it does, your positioning statement will have more credibility, and the fact that the organization provides these benefits in different areas provides proof points that support that positioning statement.

If your brand architecture uses a "house of brands," like P&G, the benefits of a new brand (as reflected by its positioning statement) need not align with the other brands in the organization's brand portfolio, because each of the brands is independent of the organization's other brands. Hence the brand's benefits can be different from those of the organization's other brands. While this might a good thing, since it offers a degree of flexibility in what the brand's benefits might be, the independence of the new brand means that the organization's other brands do not help in establishing the credibility of the new brand's positioning statement. As such, you will need to look at other strengths within the organization or value chain to see if they align with the benefits noted in the positioning statement to enhance the new brand's credibility.

OTHER CREDIBILITY DRIVERS

Organizations can also look at other aspects of their organization that may influence the credibility of the positioning statement. For example, an outstanding organizational reputation may help the perceptions you are trying to create with your positioning statement, whereas a poor reputation might hinder them.

Examine your organization's incentive structure as well. To illustrate, let's say a customer wants a set of products that work together as a "system." But in your organization, product managers care about their own products and resist changing the terms of sale of the system. Though you're selling software, the hardware is sold by a different product manager in your company. You might want to target a price-sensitive segment and thus want to lower the price of the system. But the product manager for hardware may be resistant to lowering the price, as it would go against that product manager's incentives. In this example, salespeople may shape orders that minimize cross-product orders to avoid lowered commissions or time-consuming internal interactions. For another example, imagine your positioning statement emphasizes service. If the incentive structure doesn't compensate employees for services, your ability to credibly execute on your positioning statement would be compromised. These types of incompatible incentives can make it harder to execute on your brand's positioning statement fully and credibly.

WHAT ELSE ABOUT YOUR ORGANIZATION MATTERS

There are also additional analyses, listed in Exhibit 5.2, that don't directly affect the credibility of your positioning statement but will influence your ability to execute and deliver the positioning statement's promise to the market. For example, your organization might sell another product (not the one you are currently positioning) that is targeted toward a shrinking market. This situation might put pressures on you to target a large and growing segment of the market with your brand. Extra resources might be needed to target this larger segment.

EXHIBIT 5.2

What Else About Your Organization Can Affect Your Ability to Execute and Deliver On Your Positioning Statement?
Cost analysis, such as break-even figures and margin requirement
The organization's financial stability and willingness to spend money
An organizational culture that supports marketing
The organization's history in delivering the benefits

A related issue is the organization's financial stability and its willingness to spend money on the brand you are positioning (e.g., for marketing and sales, or infrastructure expenditures in the value chain). For example, if you target a segment that is unaware of your brand, you will need to engage in advertising and other promotions to build brand awareness. Such activities can be costly, and your organization might not be willing bear high costs. You should also analyze any cannibalization issues; for instance, if another brand in your organization does well, will it eat into the sales of your brand? If so, that's a weakness that can affect your brand's success.

The culture of your organization is another area to examine. You might work in a culture that doesn't believe in spending money on marketing. Such a culture could be detrimental to executing on your positioning statement. Alternatively, your organization might have a culture of innovativeness or working together collaboratively. Such elements of your culture can affect how well you can execute on your positioning statement.

Factors such as whether you have a widely known brand name, quick-response customer service, deep knowledge of customers, robust logistical ties with suppliers, products embodying "ease of use," flexible and adaptive manufacturing, great R&D/innovation, and so on can also affect whether you can deliver on your positioning statement.

By analyzing your organization at large, you are better able to assess the credibility of your positioning statement. That is, there are factors associated with your organization that offer proof points that support it. They will also help you understand your abilities to execute on the positioning statement.

DID YOU PASS THE STRESS TEST?

If you can make a case for the strengths, and—better yet, the core competencies—supporting the benefits noted in your positioning statement, then congratulations! You've passed the stress test. You can add these strengths as proof points that support the benefits in your positioning statement and make it credible.

To demonstrate, let's examine an example of adding strengths and credibility to a positioning statement. The client, which we'll call the XYZ Company, had a product that allowed people to see in the dark. Their target segment was luxury car dealers, as the ultimate buyer was purchasers of luxury cars. The dealer segment wanted safety at a reasonable price. (Note that the ultimate customers of these cars might not care about the prices associated with luxury cars, but the dealers did, as low prices would make them more money as salespeople.)

The benefits in the positioning statement were an affordable automobile option offering high levels of safety (low price and safety). Their preliminary positioning statement was:

> For luxury car dealers, the XYZ Company provides safety at a reasonable price because we, alone among our competitors, have several years in the defense industry.

Organization analysis revealed the XYZ Company could offer these benefits because they were part of a larger organization with a long history of driving manufacturing costs down, and they had many years of defense-industry experience in safety-oriented night sight solutions. In fact, these strengths were also foundations for core competencies. As a result, the positioning statement changed to:

> For luxury car dealers, the XYZ Company provides safety at a reasonable price because we have a long history of driving manufacturing costs down, and we have many years of defense-industry experience in safety-oriented night sight solutions.

Notice how the strengths of the organization now directly map into the benefits desired by the segment. The benefit of safety is supported by the years of experience in safety-oriented night sight solutions for the defense industry. The benefit of low price is supported by their historical ability to drive manufacturing costs down. So, the second positioning statement is *far more credible* than the preliminary version, which is not focused on backing up the benefit promise. Communication messages about the product can now include the benefits as well as strong proof points from this analysis.

For a real-life example of backing up a claim of benefits with an organization's core competencies, let's look at Lucent, which Nokia later absorbed. When Lucent started, after splitting off from AT&T, they were partially in the telecommunications business, but they were also in the ideas business. They had an ad that advertised their product as, "Ideas, ideas, ideas." Now, anybody could say that they will give you great ideas. But here is how they backed up this claim: they listed some of their most successful inventions, which included the dial tone as well as the development of faxing, sound in movies, television transmission, radio astronomy, the computer, transistor, the laser . . . you get the idea.

Positioning statements are more credible when the benefits in your positioning statement are aligned with the strengths of your organization or value chain.

So, positioning statements are more credible when the benefits in a positioning statement are aligned with the strengths of an organization or value chain.

WHAT HAPPENS IF YOU DON'T PASS THE STRESS TEST?

When you don't pass the stress test, are you left with no abilities that match up to the benefits you are promising to the market (as with the benefit Entertaining to Use in Exhibit 5.1)? In this situation, you will have to ask yourself if you can credibly deliver on your positioning statement's promises. Maybe you need to give up on this benefit (and segment, if the segment strongly wants this benefit) and see if there are other segments where there is a match between the target segment's desired benefits and your organization's competencies. Alternatively, you might have time to build up your strengths now that you understand you need to match them with market benefits; or maybe you can see whether there are strengths along your value chain that might be leveraged to support that benefit. Or you might see if you can acquire these strengths from other areas in your organization, or by using joint ventures, licensing, or subcontractors.

PLAYBOOK RULE #5

Match the benefits desired by the market and your organization's strengths to gain credibility.

It is crucial to understand the importance of analyzing your organization (and associated value chain)—that is, to know thyself. The main action point for you, the reader, is to analyze your organization to see if you have the strengths (or better yet, the core competencies) that support the benefits desired by customers in your target segment—or weaknesses that could undermine them. You can change your positioning statement based on this analysis. Before moving on, let's summarize the main points.

KEY TAKEAWAYS

1. Look at your organization to see if there is a match between the benefits in your positioning statement and your organization's strengths. Use a value chain approach to give you a detailed view of your brand, including upstream and downstream activities. Matches between what the organization is good at and the benefits in the positioning statement add to the credibility of the positioning statement.
2. Examine whether your organization's brand architecture can affect what customers will think about your brand. If your organization operates as a "house of brands," a fit between the benefits of those brands and the brand in your positioning statement means that your positioning statement will be more credible. A lack of fit reduces this credibility.
3. Think about what other elements associated with your organization (reputation, finances, culture, incentive structure, etc.) might affect the credibility of your positioning statement or the extent to which you can execute on it.
4. If you've passed this stress test, go on to the next stress test, discussed in chapter six. If not, reevaluate and, if possible, revise your positioning statement by emphasizing a different target or different benefits.

PASS THE DEFENSIBILITY STRESS TEST

In chapter five, we discussed a stress test that helps you determine whether your positioning statement is *credible* based on your organization's capabilities. This chapter discusses another stress test that focuses on how *defensible* your positioning statement is. Whereas the credibility issue involves an internal focus on your organization, the defensibility issue involves an outward focus on your competitors. In essence, we are asking whether our positioning statement makes sense given how we think competitors will respond once we execute on it. In other words, to return to Sun Tzu, how well do we know our enemy?

HOW WILL COMPETITORS REACT?

Considering the defensibility of a positioning statement means thinking through how competitors will react if you go through with your proposed positioning. Competitors have incentives to take market share away from you, and one way they do this is to position themselves for strategic advantage.

Consider the positioning statement from chapter five about the organization targeting dealers of luxury cars with a low-cost, safety-oriented solution. Competitors can respond in many ways. For example, competitors could throw millions of dollars into advertising focusing on the safety of their product, with a goal of having the market believe their brand is better at safety. A competitor could also drop their price significantly so that the price advantage in your positioning statement diminishes. Competitors could launch another product aimed right at the same positioning of your brand. In addition, you might be inviting new competitors if you are positioning your brand to a target segment with few or no competitors, especially if the competitor believes there is a lot of money to be made with a similar position. In short, competitors generally don't act passively.

When thinking about how competitors might react if we follow through with our positioning statement, we are naturally thrown into thinking about a future world. We are not looking retrospectively, nor do we think about the competition in a passive way. Our perspective is different from the way most people talk about competition. We adopt this active and future-oriented perspective by considering competitive reactions as a dynamic game.

You might ask why we frame competition as a dynamic game. Well, think of a price war, in which competitors drop their prices in reaction to competitors dropping their prices, as in the 1992 competition between American Airlines, Northwest Airlines, and other U.S. airlines. One airline would lower its prices, which caused another to lower its prices, which in turn caused further price reductions. Commodities are often prone to price wars, given their tendency to emphasize price alone. These are overt examples of dynamic games between competitors in a market.

We also think about competition as a dynamic game because there is an entire subdiscipline of academics that uses game theory to effectively study how competitive markets act and react.[1] We propose that you consider any competitive moves as a game since participants react to each other's movements, even if the actions are subtler than those in a price war.

We mentioned competitors in chapter one, where we talked about how companies compete on benefits (such as the way that Uber competed with taxis on the same core benefits but added additional benefits that customers wanted). But unlike regimented games like chess, with strict rules and just one competitor at a time, brands in unregulated markets often have multiple competitors that can act freely and simultaneously—and you might have unknown competitors too. In order to respond well to competition in this type of environment, we encourage you to play the type of game we discuss in this chapter, which involves considering the likelihood of competitors' reactions if you go through with your proposed positioning statement.

Of course, you might be able to avoid competition if you use traditional barriers that keep competitors at bay. Trademarks, patents, government policy, mastery of technology, economies of scale, learning curves, access to distribution channels, a great brand, and customer delight are all examples of barriers to entry. Notice the final barrier is customer delight. Yes, if you do everything to delight your customers, you may be able to keep competitors out. If you have developed a highly admired brand, this can also keep competitors out (more on brand admiration in chapter nine). Short of this, you need to accept competition as part of your marketing strategy.

Let's begin the stress test by getting into the challenging problem of identifying the competition.

IDENTIFYING THE COMPETITION

On the surface, identifying the competition may sound easy, since you have already targeted a segment and likely know the other organizations that have targeted the same segment. However, competitors can enter by providing new or enhanced benefits, as we showed in chapter one. Moreover, as competitive strategist Michael Porter has shown, competition can come from many places.[2] While organizations tend to think of their core competition as coming from existing competitors, suppliers to your industry can "forward integrate" and become new competitors. For example, a manufacturer that sells to retailers may decide to go around them and sell directly to end customers. If you are a retailer, the company that used to be a part of your supply chain is now your competitor. Additionally, some buyers can "integrate backward," such as by buying another organization that supplies the brands or services needed for production. Porter also talks about competition from new entrants to the market and substitute products (these are products from a different industry that offer similar benefits as the products produced by organizations within the industry). But if you follow our advice and stay focused on customer benefits, you will be able to take note of these entrants and substitutes before they wreak havoc on your organization. You will also be able to see which of your competitors are direct competitors (those that emphasize the same benefits for their brand that you plan to emphasize) and which are indirect competitors (those that focus on other market segments who want different benefits).

In some cases, your competitors may also be partners you are working with. For example, maybe customers need two products to work together to get value from either product. If you have hired someone to redesign your kitchen, for instance, your designer might tell you that your redesign will require an electrician—and that they work with electricians and can handle this problem for you. In this case, the designer is the prime contractor, and they hire electricians as subcontractors. This is a very common situation in many industries, including the defense industry, where complex systems are bought by the government. In situations like this, competition can arise between the prime and subcontractors, as the subcontractors may try to become prime contractors and take business away from the other prime contractors.

If you follow our advice and stay focused on customer benefits, you will be able to take note of these entrants and substitutes before they wreak havoc on your organization.

And these are just a few of the variety of forms competition can come in!

At first, you might narrow your view of competition by focusing on direct competitors, then other competitors in the market, and then other competitors that might enter your market (e.g., substitutes). For the immediate purpose of a stress test on your positioning statement, consider all current competitors in the segment you are targeting, then choose the two strongest and one less apparent competitor for further analysis. To determine these competitors, you can also use the perceptual map we discussed in chapter two, which will show you your competition from a customer's perspective.

FINDING COMPETITIVE INFORMATION

Subjecting your positioning statement to a stress test for defensibility requires a proactive stance toward the competition. To achieve this bold stance, you will need competitive information. There are a great many sources of competitive intelligence. These sources include mission statements, press analyses, trade interviews, marketing communications to customers, and launches of new brands, among other available data. Such information is public, easy to find, and can be tracked systematically with the Internet. If you have access to a company like LexisNexis, which sells data analytics products and databases, you can find information on patents, partnerships, industry reports, and more. If your competitor is a public organization, much of their strategy is public information. Go to sites that comment on public organizations (e.g., the Motley Fool) and investment sites (such as Charles Schwab), and you'll find much helpful information.[3] You can find a lot of relevant information on your competitors on the internet.[4] Changes in what a competitor does are also informative, because they tell you what new things a competitor has decided to do.

You can also talk to customers who are likely to know important information about your competitors—since they probably considered purchasing from them in the past. You can also consider the situation as an investor (would you invest in your competitor's business?). Thinking as an interested investor motivates you to determine the strengths and weaknesses of your competitors.

You likely have people in your organization who can provide helpful competitive information too. But there may be barriers to gathering and processing competitive intelligence. Working with large defense contractors taught us how easy it was for groups to evolve into silos that kept competitive intelligence locked up. Look to people in your organization who might have access to such information.

Finally, use the Internet and search engines to find various types of organizational information. Check keywords for search engines, pay-per-click advertising, and more. Sign up for your competitor's newsletter if they have one. Nowadays, various automated services, like Crayon, use AI-driven analysis and machine learning based on data they capture for you about your competitors.

With tools like these, getting information on your competitors is much easier now than it was in the past.

USING COMPETITIVE INFORMATION FOR PREDICTION

We've seen organizations that say they do competitive intelligence but rarely use it proactively. They gather competitive information and put together competitive profiles and battlecards (one-page visual aids comparing an organization's pricing, product, features, etc., to a competitor's). This is good, but it's not the proactive approach we advocate.

As we've said before, you need to play a dynamic game if you want to succeed. Using the competitive information you have gathered, you need to predict what the competition will do if you move forward with your proposed positioning. To do this, organize your competitive information into two categories:

- *Ability*—Do your identified competitors have the resources to react to your positioning (e.g., with money for advertising)?
- *Motivation*—How motivated are they to respond? Such motivation is a combination of the competitor's objectives and strategy. Would reacting be consistent with their financial objectives? Would responding be consistent with their business and marketing strategy?

Why do you need to assess both the ability and motivation of the competition to act in response to your proposed positioning statement? Because to act, an organization must have both components. A competitor with high ability but little motivation, or a competitor with motivation but no ability, likely would not be a problem for your company if you were to target and position in a segment where they were a player.

Using the competitive information you have gathered, you need to predict what the competition will do if you move forward with your proposed positioning.

Ability

Use the information you have gathered to uncover the abilities of a competitor. Using the luxury car safety positioning statement from chapter five, imagine that you are looking for evidence that your competitors can provide both high levels of safety and a low price. So, any evidence that a competitor has the capacity to deliver higher levels of safety would be relevant, as would be any evidence they can support a low price now or in the future.

We are primarily interested in whether competitors can penetrate the segment we are targeting and whether they will try to increase market perceptions of safety and low price for their own brands. You can refer to various value chain activities for their brands for clues. As for upstream activities, check if the competitor is known for buying low-cost components, which might compromise their ability to provide high safety levels but would provide a lower-cost product. For downstream activities, analyze their skills in identifying current and future customer needs, focusing on brand development and how creative their marketing communications are.

To assess whether a competitor currently targeting a different segment has the strategy to move into your targeted segment, you can use the value chain framework from the last chapter to see how their strategy aligns with the strengths and weaknesses associated with their value chain.

Motivation

Our goal here is to obtain information that will help you identify your competitors' objectives and strategies, which together compose their motivation to respond to your positioning statement. The classic objectives are financial—that is, how willing your competitor is to invest in its business. Typical measures include market share, sales growth, and profit objectives. Again, you are looking for any objectives and strategies that relate to your proposed positioning statement.

Strategies cover where they are planning to go. For example, do they want to be a leading brand in safety? Do they aim to be known as the premier service organization or the premier safety organization? Such information will indicate what "turf" they are likely to defend.

PLAYING OUT A GAME

Allen has taught dynamic competitive analysis in executive education programs as well as at huge companies like Northrop Grumman. Before getting to the game, he draws the graph in Exhibit 6.1 on the board and then asks the participants a question.

EXHIBIT 6.1

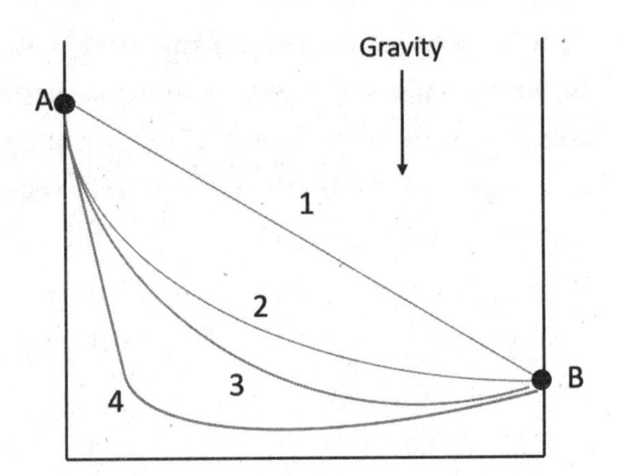

Imagine a small ball with a hole placed it at point A. You thread the hole with a flexible wire that can be configured in an infinite variety of different ways. The numbers (1, 2, 3, 4) represent just four example paths of the wire (examples of the paths the small ball can take). Using only the force of gravity and the path of the wire with no friction, the objective is to get the ball to point B as fast as possible. Which of the four paths, or any other path, represents the fastest way to get from point A to point B?

This question is known as the brachistochrone problem and was first posed by Johann Bernoulli in 1696.[5] Which is the best path? Many people choose path 1. Now, that is a straight line and solves a different problem; namely, the *shortest distance* between points A and B. Other people choose path 4, thinking that gravity would help you reach the fastest speed at the beginning, and then you could quickly zip over to point B. But it is not possible to find the solution to the problem when you take a forward-looking view. You can only solve the problem mathematically by moving backward from point B to point A—determining via integral calculus which path is fastest.

In other words, to optimize the path going forward (i.e., the configuration of the flexible wire), you need to optimize by starting at the end of the problem and working backward. If this seems odd to you, consider the words of ice hockey star Wayne Gretzky: "I skate to where the puck is going, not where it has been."

The optimal way to frame your competitive decisions and actions when dealing with a competitor is to start at the end of the game instead of starting at the beginning. Unfortunately, most of us don't have the mental skills to systematically think backward. Still, we can iteratively move forward and think through the end of the game until we find an optimal path. This is precisely what we are going to do next.

This stress test evaluates whether your positioning statement remains robust in the face of competitive moves.

We will use the preceding competitor analyses to frame a game and predict what your competitor will do now that you have selected a target segment and developed a positioning statement. This stress test evaluates whether your positioning statement remains robust in the face of competitive moves. Assume your target segment cares the most about ease of use, and thus you have positioned your product as the easiest to use. How would a competitor react to this positioning? What would you do in reaction to the competitive move? How would competitor react to your move? And so on.

Just like playing any dynamic competitive game (e.g., hockey, football), you need to understand your competitor's abilities and motivation (i.e., their strategy and objectives). Fortunately, if you did the hard work presented in chapter five and gathered the competitive intelligence described in this chapter, you should be ready.

Role-play your responses to competition with two teams. One team plays your organization. The other takes the competitor's side. See if you can get other people in your organization involved (though you can do this individually if you don't have two teams—it's just less fun). To see how this might play out, consider this situation in our example—you're the organization whose stated position is safety at a low price. Here are the steps of the game:

1. Will the competitor respond?
    - Refer to their motivation.
2. How effective will the response be?
    - Refer to their motivation and their abilities.
3. Do you have an effective counter-response?
    - What are your strengths and competencies?
4. How would they respond to your counter-response?
5. Do you have an effective counter-counter-response?

6. How would they respond to your counter-counter-response?
7. . . . And so on.

Play out the entire game in your mind before you spend precious resources on your strategy and figure out only later that you have played a losing hand. If you play out a game and you lose, try again with a different set of moves. For example, let's say you start by positioning in a certain segment, but without spending much in advertising to build awareness. And then you predict your competitor would start advertising a little. OK . . . so, what would happen if you invested a huge amount of money in advertising? Would the game change?

What you're looking for is an endgame in which you are confident that your positioning statement is defensible given how competitors are likely to react. Practically speaking, you can usually see the end of the game after just a few moves.

What you're looking for is an endgame in which you are confident that your positioning statement is defensible given how competitors are likely to react.

If you find that competition will make it hard for you to position yourself as you intended, you may want to rethink your targeting and positioning decisions (as described in chapter four). Alternatively, if you have identified your core competencies (chapter five), you may consider staying the course and offering higher levels of the benefits that customers want. In fact, that's precisely what XYZ Company (whose positioning statement featured in chapter five) did with their positioning statement. Their credibility was so high that it kept their competition from making any serious challenges to their positioning. So, a highly credible positioning statement can enhance its own defensibility.

Finally, you may have some assumptions about your competitor's actions (even unprovoked ones) in the future. If so, play out the game based on these assumptions as we describe next.

WHAT ABOUT ASSUMPTIONS?

The competitor analysis and the gaming process described in the previous section sometimes rely on making some assumptions. Assumptions are not a problem. Marketing, just like every other discipline in business, makes assumptions. The data for artificial intelligence is messy, competitors and our organizations don't act as expected, there are uncertain interest rates, culture changes . . . there is never complete certainty.

Even other business functions like finance and accounting make assumptions. To see this, consider putting together a capital sufficiency model for yourself. This model is Accounting and Finance 101 and can help you see how much money you will have in the future. You first need to make assumptions about interest rates, inflation rates, rates of return, etc. Though these are hard numbers, they are based on assumptions—and the finance department in your organization makes similar assumptions. They'll say they use net present value for a certain calculation. But net present value involves discounting cash flows that arise in the future. So, they must make assumptions about interest rates in the future. If they could actually accurately predict interest rates in the future, they wouldn't be working for your organization—because they could make billions of dollars betting on interest rate futures. The key is to make assumptions that are well supported and *likely* to be true, even if perfect accuracy is impossible.

You simply need to be careful with your assumptions. If the defensibility of your positioning statement hinges on many assumptions being correct, then you should question its viability, since it rests on shaky ground. Test out your competitor predictions against these assumptions with "what ifs." Move forward with your positioning statement if you reach the same conclusion even when making different assumptions. In this way, dynamic competitive analysis will reveal insights you can use going forward.

Marketing and other business functions like finance and accounting make assumptions. Test out your competitor predictions against these assumptions with "what ifs."

Finally, some readers might wonder if the stress tests in chapters five and six could be performed before the targeting decision and positioning statements have been constructed. The answer is yes. You have flexibility in the order of these stress tests. However, by putting the stress tests after targeting and positioning your brand, the tests are much more focused on making sure you have a credible and defensible position in the market.

DID YOU PASS THE STRESS TESTS?

After your positioning statement has passed the stress tests, you now have a credible and defensible positioning. If your statement didn't pass the stress test, then reconsider the recommendations of these past two chapters, including rethinking your selected target segment and positioning statement.

Once you're ready to move forward, put together a final positioning statement for each segment you plan to target, and use these points to see if it works. In a successful final positioning statement,

- the content is clear, credible, and relevant;
- yours company can attain it;
- it matches your strengths and has internal support; and
- it is distinctive and difficult for future competitors to copy.

The next step is to focus on improving the attributes and features that will give rise to the benefits noted in your positioning statement. When we introduced benefits, we focused on benefits first and attributes and features later. Now is the time to think about attributes and features, because by changing them you will more readily deliver on the benefit promised in your positioning statement.

Once you have a positioning statement, you can also go back to your perceptual map and see what you need to do to move your current position into your intended position. Gaps can be closed by either changing "reality" (e.g., improving or changing attributes and features) or changing "perceived reality" (e.g., investing in communications that promote the benefits).

PLAYBOOK RULE #6

Play out dynamic games to see if your targeting decision and positioning statement are defensible or not.

Now that you've learned about competitive analysis, the main action point for you, the reader, is to gather information on competitors and game out your competitors, using the approach outlined in this chapter. See if your positioning statement is defensible or needs to change. Before moving on, let's summarize the main points.

KEY TAKEAWAYS

1. It is important to stress-test your positioning by considering how defensible it is against competitors' potential reactions to it.
2. Do not think about competition in a passive, reactive manner. Think dynamically and prospectively by playing out a game.
3. You must know your competitors' motivation and abilities to play the game. There is information available on objectives, strategies, and tools to help you turn this knowledge into competitive intelligence.
4. When simulating competition via a game, focus on the target segment and benefits noted in your positioning statement and the competitors that are operating in the same segment. Play out the game to the end. If you lose, it's no problem. Try it again with a different set of moves. Consider the sequential moves of your competitors if you were to execute on your positioning statement. Remember, this is a mental game, and you have squandered no resources.
5. After passing the stress tests from chapters five and six, you can move on to focusing on the features and attributes that directly correspond to the benefits in your positioning statement.

REPLAY—A CASE STUDY

In this chapter, we present a case study, rooted in one of Allen's experiences, that illustrates the ideas in the previous chapters. Allen had been consulting and teaching at a large multinational semiconductor chip company for a few years when he unexpectedly received an email from the president of the company's European division. The short email said, "Teach my people to say no." Upon follow-up email exchanges, Allen learned that the president was referring to the tendency of the company's salespeople to spread themselves too thin by trying to sell to everybody in the semiconductor chip market, including customers who had no interest in their product. He wanted Allen to show them how to segment the market and focus on the most viable target segments.

This is a common problem among organizations that do not segment their markets on benefits. Organizations often just focus on getting whoever is willing to buy what they are selling without realizing this is a wasteful practice. The reason why is that a lot of the effort is devoted to potential customers who will never actually buy (as the president intimated). Allen was impressed that this president of a major corporation looked beyond common business behaviors and realized how wasteful this nondirected practice can be.

A few weeks later, Allen had flown to Frankfurt, Germany, to meet with the company's senior executive staff and explain his perspective on segmenting a market and positioning brands. Essentially, the president wanted Allen to develop an "invasion plan" for entering what he called the "middle market" for their brand of computer chips in Europe. Historically, this company had approached the semiconductor chip market like others with a sales force focused on the top tier (e.g., the large cell phone companies), essentially neglecting everybody else. In addition to the problem of inefficient sales work, another of the president's main concerns was that the next high-growth company would likely arise from this tremendous middle market of smaller companies. He would say that the next Steve Jobs was in a garage out there in the middle market, and if his computer chip company didn't pay any attention to this part of the market, one of his competitors would.

After being introduced to the executives in the meeting, Allen started by asking them a simple question: What benefits did the executives believe customers in this middle market considered when purchasing from them versus one of the many competitors? On the whiteboard, Allen started listing their benefits, which included performance, how easy it was for developers to use the chip, and several other benefits.

Price was also included (of course). It was clear to Allen that the executives had never thought about a benefit perspective on the market.

Allen then asked the executives if any buyers in the middle market cared mainly about performance, including using technical applications that needed high performance. The room then launched into a discussion about all the buyers they had encountered that mostly cared about the chip's performance. They could even name applications that used chips in this group of customers. Allen asked if there were buyers who mainly cared about ease of use (e.g., providing technical documentation). Another discussion erupted about buyers who mainly cared about ease of use, with examples of buyers of chips and their technological applications.

Allen then explained that this was a very simple demonstration of segmentation of benefits. He then explained more about benefits, what perceptual maps would reveal, and how this could lead to targeting, positioning, and implementing an entire strategically viable marketing plan.

The process Allen led them through is the same as what we've discussed in this book so far. The president believed in using benefits as the driving force for this engagement. While other computer chip companies focused on chip size as the basis for segmentation, the president saw a keen opportunity to discern what the middle market actually wanted, thus getting a leg up on competitors. Once the company understood how this market was segmented, they could decide how to enter this market strategically.

This chapter retells the main points from all the previous chapters in a case study that led to a positioning statement in one segment of the market and a strategy for the entire market. Though this case study is from a specific high-level consulting engagement, we will keep the description general. This case study is relevant not only to technology companies or companies in similar situations to this one—we also have used the same process with music companies, insurance companies, banks, and more. The point is that *benefits transcend all industries.* All customers want benefits independent of industry or any other classification system you use.

THE CONTEXT AND PROCESS

Upon returning from his trip, Allen learned that the executive team wanted to move forward with this engagement. Over the next few weeks, Allen worked with a colleague to outline the details of the consulting work. The client decided the engagement would entail working with fifty marketing and sales personnel. It would take place over five days in Germany, and six weeks later, over another five days in France. Because of two challenges, the consulting engagement would take far longer than the typical positioning engagement Allen has led. First, the engagement included team-building—bringing together groups who worked in different divisions and countries. Second, the goal was to attain consensus for the positioning plan among all the parties involved, since they would oversee the implementation process, though Allen was concerned only with the positioning and was not personally involved with any part of the implementation phase of this project.

Before the first meeting, Allen and his colleague met with senior management and settled on the buying context. Specifically, the buying context was a "design win," meaning that the goal was to get a buyer not only to try out a chip but also, more important, to design it into their system, thereby locking in a long-term purchase. The buyer, in this case, could be a very small company or even a larger growing company. They also decided that the design would be a computer chip and the logic board that accompanied it. In this way, the buyer was essentially buying a system. Specifying the buying context is a critical step to positioning, since it determines how customers choose between all the options on the market. Gaining consensus about the system was important (and challenging), because half the group came from the semiconductor side of the company while the other half was responsible for the logic board.

THE FIRST WEEK

The team met for the first week of work in Frankfurt. Allen started the meeting by explaining the context of the task; namely, that the product of focus was defined as a chip with a logic board. It came to be known as the chip solution. An overview of the entire process was then provided, and Allen finished with an explanation of the concept of benefits. Ideally, the group would identify benefits using techniques described in chapter one. But given the problem at hand and timing constraints, it was decided that the group would first use the managerial approach to identifying benefits and then later collect empirical data from customers to see if they were missing any benefits (chapter three details these two approaches). The plan was for the group to do all the analyses and then test their assumptions with real customers during the ensuing six-week break.

The participants then worked in teams of five to seven people to outline their understanding of the benefits sought by the middle market, especially in the context of a system-level buy (the chip and the logic board). This task was made easier since the group included salespeople who had spent much time with customers.

When the teams finished identifying the benefits, they had a list of about ten benefits that composed the market, with clear definitions for each benefit. The teams made sure that the benefits were distinct from one another, so that no two benefits would be redundant. For example, the group identified two types of support-related benefits (product support and systems applications support), but after they defined these benefits, it became clear that they were distinct benefits and not highly correlated. The definitions also made it easier for the group to discuss these benefits later and saved them from needing to revisit the benefits repeatedly.

Shocks to the industry needed to be considered as well. Due to fires in various chip production factories, manufacturers had problems fulfilling orders (a type of shock described in chapter one), which was especially salient because one of the benefits in this market was what they called "fulfillment" (the availability and delivery of computer chips and logic boards).

Allen then explained benefit segmentation (as in chapter three). To help everyone get started, Allen gave the teams several hints, based on his prior experience, on how one might segment this market on benefits.

As the teams worked, they engaged in several lively discussions. One major question was whether cost/price was table stakes in this market or not. There was a great deal of disagreement on this subject, but ultimately, the group decided that cost/price was more relevant to certain parts of the market than others and, hence, was not a table stakes requirement.

Through discussions like these, the group finally came to a consensus on how this market was segmented. Everyone agreed this market had three distinct segments. In addition, the salespeople readily identified a few specific applications for the product (e.g., military radar systems, barcode readers, graphics accelerators, musical instruments, Dolby sound) for each segment. These applications were vital, since they acted as "descriptors" for the segments. Thus, later, if we decided on a segment to target, everyone knew the types of applications in that segment.

The group named the three segments—"Innovators," "Pragmatists," and "Quick & Easy" (which you may recognize from chapter four). The Innovators were primarily interested in the benefit of high performance. The Pragmatists wanted a balance of performance for a reasonable price, and the Quick & Easy segment wanted the benefits of ease of use and technical support. As you can see, the segments primarily cared about two or three benefits, due to the trade-offs we discussed in chapter three. As a result, several market benefits, such as fulfillment, did not significantly affect the segmentation. That some benefits do not affect the segmentation is typical when segmenting by benefits.

Before concluding the first week, the entire group worked to create provisional perceptual maps based on their best understanding of how the market viewed their company and four of its competitors. This was made easier again because of the sales personnel's direct contact with customers in the middle market. They aimed to reduce bias by making it clear that they were not interested in what they personally believed, but rather their knowledge of how customers in the market perceived each brand.

While they had not tested the perceptual maps with real customers yet, it became clear at this point that the company would have difficulties entering all three market segments. For one, their brand was not perceived to be easy to use, as the Quick & Easy segment wanted. Part of this was a historical lack of easy-to-read technical documentation for their computer chips, especially compared with one of their competitors, which had invested heavily in such documentation. Despite this awareness, the decision to target segments was not going to take place during this first session, since they needed to test some of the group's assumptions in the market. Since they hadn't yet tested the segmentation and perceptual maps on real customers, it was possible the concerns about being unable to enter all segments were unwarranted.

TESTING THE ANALYSIS WITH THE MARKET

During the next six weeks, the group returned to their home offices, which were spread throughout Europe, and met with potential customers in the middle market. They showed these customers the benefit segmentation and the perceptual map and asked for any changes the customers would make to either analysis. Since most customers had never seen a perceptual map, this required some explanation.

The teams also gathered estimated market size and growth data for the entire European chip industry and at the level of each of the three segments. To do this, they employed basic assumptions about the size of the entire European chip market and how it would continue to develop over time. The projected five-year compound average growth rate for the three segments was 8 percent for the Innovators, 25 percent for the Pragmatists, and 64 percent for the Quick and Easy segment. As the growth rates suggest, this market was like many tech markets in that sales started with Innovators, spread to Pragmatists, and then eventually spread to the Quick & Easy users too.

THE SECOND WEEK

When everyone reconvened in France, the perceptual maps created in the first week were updated to incorporate what the group had learned from speaking with actual customers—and, fortunately, the segmentation did not change. The original perceptual map was similar to the final map, which reinforced a belief that the group was on the right track. Allen then moved on to the targeting decision.

Based on all the preceding analyses, the group formulated a targeting plan. They looked at segment size, growth rates, the investment required, and whether targeting one segment would make moving into another segment easier. First, it was clear that the Quick & Easy segment was growing the fastest but was dense with serious competition. Second, the perceptual map showed that the company was perceived to have the performance desired by the Innovator segment.

TARGET SEGMENT, POSITIONING STATEMENT, AND STRESS TESTS

The company's preliminary decision was to target all three segments one at a time, given resource limitations. The group then created positioning statements that stated their promises to each segment of the market.

Allen also worked with the group on the company and competitor analysis. It was clear that the company had a lot of competition in the Quick & Easy segment. One of their major competitors had forgone cutting-edge performance for ease of use, which is a fairly typical market strategy. As for the company itself, the group focused on their ability to provide the market benefits—the benefits-strengths analysis we discussed in chapter five. They also focused on the competitor's motivations and abilities. This analysis made it easy to game out the targeting decision and positioning statement later (in the way we discussed in chapter six).

Fortunately, this company had core competencies for performance (e.g., they were the inventor of the particular chip we focused on and had the leading architecture for design and innovation of the chip) that matched the benefits desired by the Innovators, making an updated positioning statement easy to create. However, they did not have the current strengths to support the benefits expected by the Quick & Easy segment. They planned to focus on building strengths to support this benefit in the future, and mapped out next steps for improving market perceptions of those benefits.

The competitive games stress tests revealed they could enter the segments as planned—that is, over time, once they had built up the strengths needed to enter and defend their position in the different segments.

The output from this workshop was a thirty-two-page PowerPoint presentation, put together by the teams, that outlined a complete invasion strategy for the middle market (Exhibit 7.1). Appointed members of the group presented the plan to senior management with a recommended strategy and two alternatives.

EXHIBIT 7.1. Invasion Strategy

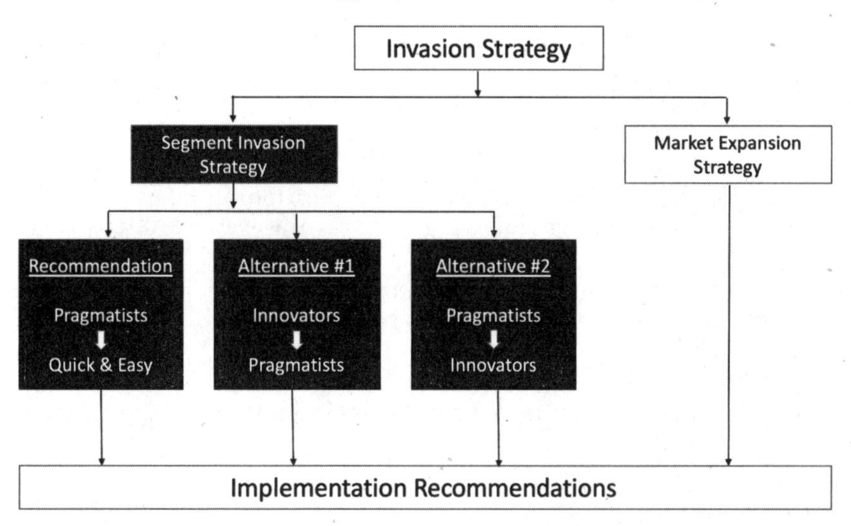

The group also created a table that presented a full list of every application associated with each segment. These applications are an example of descriptors, as we talked about in chapter three. Once the group decided on the targeting plan, they'd immediately know which types of applications (and thus companies) they would be targeting. In addition, they recommended a middle-market "product" that was robust, automated, and wide ranging, since they now realized how important support was for the strategic invasion plan.

The rest was execution, especially how this company would make the promises specified in the positioning statements come alive.

PLAYBOOK RULE #7

To identify the benefits of the market, start with creating internal alignment with your entire team.

KEY TAKEAWAYS

1. It is essential to get as many people involved in the positioning process as possible. Not only is consensus about the positioning necessary to gain a shared understanding, but implementing the promises inherent in the positioning takes the entire team. This is particularly important since you need to communicate benefits throughout the customer journey (as we describe in chapter eight).
2. People can look objectively at the market when appropriately guided. If not guided appropriately, they will get biased information.
3. Appreciate the power of a target migration strategy. It's much better to think dynamically about targeting. It conserves resources (you don't have to advertise everywhere) and allows you to build benefits wanted by other segments, so that when you do enter, you're not coming in disadvantaged.

ACTIVATE ON BENEFITS

At this point, you have done the hard work of identifying and segmenting the market, developing a perceptual map, selecting one or more target segments, and deriving credible and defensible brand positioning statements for the targeted segment(s). This chapter shows you how to activate your positioning statement(s) and bring them alive through your marketing actions. In chapter two, we argued that benefits live in brands. In this chapter, we extend this argument by showing how marketing actions can make those benefits real to customers and close any gap between how you want customers to perceive your brand (as in your positioning statement) and how they actually perceive it (based on your marketing actions).

CREATING A MESSAGE PLATFORM

Activating a positioning statement means turning the finalized positioning statement into marketing actions that communicate this positioning to target customers. This process starts by creating a message platform.

What Is a Message Platform?

Formally, a **message platform** is a written document that includes (a) background information regarding the brand in its competitive context; (b) a description of the target segment and who they are; (c) the positioning statement, which indicates what target customers care about and the brand's associated benefits, along with proof points from the stress tests that support the statement's credibility and defensibility (see chapters five and six on stress tests); and finally (d) examples of compelling and awesome messages based on the positioning statement.

The message platform is the master document that directs all touchpoints related to the brand's proposed position. By **touchpoints,** we mean all encounters that customers have with your brand from any source. In other words, all touchpoints, whether in the form of the brand name,[1] its logo, tagline,[2] advertising, content marketing, sales messages, customer service operations, and packaging, distribution, product features, and price should conform to this platform and reinforce the benefits noted in your positioning statement. If your brand is a retail brand, store signage, merchandising, store layout, and employee uniforms should also conform to this platform. If your organization is involved in merchandise delivery, delivery vehicles and their signage should also conform to the platform. If your organization is a nonprofit,

T-shirts, literature, and your website should conform to the platform. Customers' encounters with your brand should be considered vehicles for your message platform.

The Value of a Message Platform

Your message platform guides all touchpoints that customers have with your brand so that they speak with one voice and in the same language. In this way, all touchpoints are truly "integrated" and synergistic. The message platform also ensures that all touchpoints are focused, so that the key points that target customers care about are clear and not diluted. The message platform can save time internally, because everyone in your organization is on the same page about how the brand is positioned and to whom. The message platform also provides vital information to suppliers like advertising agencies and other marketing services that are involved in the brand's communication efforts. In such cases, the message platform ensures that external players will have the same understanding about the brand, its benefits, its target segment, and how these benefits are credible and defensible.

Your message platform guides all touchpoints that customers have with your brand so that they speak with one voice and in the same language.

You can use different forms of communication to execute on the message platform. For example, you might want to engage in storytelling for some communications with customers. You can be as creative as you wish with storytelling—but it's important to ensure the key benefits are apparent at some point in the story. Elsewise, the story might be compelling, but it won't connect with what targeted customers want. That's the goal of the message platform. If you don't actualize your positioning through all touchpoints, you won't have much hope of changing customers' perceptions as you promised in your brand's positioning statement.

The Message Platform and the Target Segment

As we mentioned above, the message platform should also include detailed information about who your target customers are so that they can be appropriately reached through various media channels. Recall from chapter three that when segmenting the market on benefits, we use descriptors that tell us more about who customers in the target segment are. This information will help your organization determine how to best reach customers in the targeted segment. For example, if your target segment has a large percentage of customers in a certain age range (e.g., twenty-five to thirty-four) you will want your message content to appear in the media they use, the social media sites they visit, the streaming content they watch, the podcasts they listen to, etc. Such information is essential to the message platform, as it will guide media planners (who decide which specific media to use) and media buyers (who buy ad space and ensure that ads are delivered), if your organization uses them. Fortunately, all social media sites offer targeting on a variety of demographics, including age and gender. The more descriptors you can associate with your targeted segment, the easier it will be to find appropriate communication channels.

In a B2B context, if the segment is characterized in terms of verticals, then your efforts will focus on those verticals, but not necessarily on all customers in those verticals. For example, assume your target segment uses your product or service category in a mission-critical way (meaning, if the product doesn't work as expected, the customer's business will suffer). Instead of going after the entire vertical, your sales and marketing communication should emphasize those customers in all the verticals who use your product category in a mission-critical way. Once you start thinking this way, you'll be able to think of specific customers and be able to target them using specific ads—for example, LinkedIn ads. If you have a list of current customers who are part of your target segment, consider using LinkedIn's lookalike audiences. This tool allows you to upload information about customers so as to identify other customers with similar needs.

EXAMINING THE CUSTOMER JOURNEY

In our experience, organizations often try to communicate to the market (e.g., drive traffic to their website or get more leads at the top of the conversion funnel) before thinking about the customer journey. The **customer journey** is the process between customers' first exposure to your product and the point where they have experienced and considered repurchasing your brand.

Steps in the Customer Journey

A typical customer journey involves several, typically sequential, steps:[3]

- **Problem Recognition:** Customers realize they need something that delivers certain benefits. For example, customers might realize that they need a vacation (see Exhibit 8.1 on page 171). But where to go? That's the role of information search.
- **Information Search:** Customers search for any brands that might be relevant given the benefits they seek in a product.

This is the "research and planning" stage of Exhibit 8.1. Information search can be *external,* such as when customers search online or when they gather information from others. When information search is external, an essential issue for organizations is *gaining attention* so that one's brand stands out from the clutter of other externally provided information. Information search can also be *internal,* such as when customers identify brands that might work for them from their memory. If information search is memory-based, your organization needs to consider enhancing customers' *recall of your brand* so that once problem recognition occurs, your brand immediately pops into mind.

- **Consideration Set Formation:** Customers assess which offerings are contenders for purchase based on what they have learned from your messaging and information they have heard from others. Getting your organization's brand into the customer's consideration set is a significant step toward the next step: choice. If your brand doesn't make it into the customer's consideration set, you have no hope of being chosen. Thus, an important issue that your organization should emphasize at this stage is making sure that customers' information about your product is consistent with how customers will evaluate alternatives in their consideration set.
- **Choice:** At the point of choice, customers engage in brand purchase. Customers select (purchase) the brand from their consideration set that has done the best job of convincing them that the brand is right for them. Typically, customers will choose the offering for which they have the strongest and most positive brand attitude.

- **Experience:** When customers buy and use your brand, they gain usage experience with it. Organizations that rely on subscription pricing (e.g., a gym) put a lot of emphasis on this usage stage, since if the customer doesn't use it, they are unlikely to pay the next installment of the subscription contract.
- **Postpurchase Evaluation:** After purchasing and experiencing the product, customers evaluate whether they made the right decision. The extent to which the brand (and the brand's promises) meets or exceeds customers' expectations is an integral part of this step. This stage is critical, since customers often share their brand experiences with others in online reviews (e.g., on Amazon) or other forms of social media. Negative brand experiences tend to be shared more with others, and they are likely to be highly persuasive. Hence, it is important that the customers' experiences at all the previous stages be positive.
- **Repurchase:** When customers' choices and postpurchase evaluations are very positive, they may choose the same brand again when the need arises. Repurchasing represents a form of brand loyalty. Since it costs organizations less money to promote a brand to existing customers than new ones, enhancing repurchase likelihood can be highly cost-efficient.

Customer journeys can take a little or a long time, depending on how much risk (economic risk, performance risk, psychological risk) is involved in the purchase and how familiar customers are with the offering. In some cases, as with impulse purchases, very little consideration may be made when deciding whether to purchase the product. However, when deciding on where to go on vacation, there is likely to be much more risk and thus more consideration. Similarly, many B2B purchases can take several months or longer. Hence, the customer journey can be quite long and must be thought through by your organization.

The customer journey in many B2B markets tends to start with "demand generation." Demand generation is the term used for activities used to drive awareness and interest in an organization's products. In essence, organizations are trying to take control of the process customers go through on their customer journey. To do this, many focus on "lead magnets." **Lead magnets** are something free that entices customers to act. For example, an organization might offer a free report or webinar in return for the customer's email address and other information. At this point, the organization tries to assist the customer through the stages of the customer journey using marketing automation campaigns—campaigns that are managed by technologies, across multiple channels, automatically.

Illustrating the Customer Journey

Let's walk through an example of a customer journey. Assume you work for Marriott Hotels and are working on the journey people take when looking for a hotel at which to stay on vacation. You have the following five steps in mind as your understanding of a vacationer's natural buying sequence: (1) dreaming of where to go, (2) research/planning to identify where to stay, (3) selecting and booking the right hotel, (4) stay/experience of the hotel, and (5) post-stay/reflecting on how the vacation went. Exhibit 8.1 illustrates the processes described earlier (such as problem recognition and choice), the information customers need at each stage, the touchpoints they will encounter that bear on their journey, and the content most relevant to the questions they have at each stage of the journey.

EXHIBIT 8.1. Information Needs, Touchpoints, and Content Along a Customer Journey

Customer Journey	Dreaming (Problem Recognition)	Research/Planning (Information Search and Consideration)	Booking (Choice)	Stay/ Experiencing (Experience)	Post-Stay/ Reflecting (Post-Purchase Evaluation)
Customer Question **(Type of Information Needed)**	Where can we go?	How much will it cost? (Price) What does it have to offer? (Benefits)	How do we Finalize our choices? (Information that confirms choice)	What is this really like? (Is it good or bad?)	Was it really that good? (What was the experience really like?)
Touchpoints **(Where Customers Encounter This Information)**	Travel brochures Ads Search engines	Travel agents Website for the destination Tripadvisor reviews	Booking via the web Booking through an agent	Destination personnel (staff) Destination ambience/ atmosphere	Invitations to write reviews Follow-up call post-trip
Content Focus and *Communication Objectives*	Create content that enhances *brand name awareness*	Create content that fosters *brand knowledge, consideration set formation*, based on the brand's benefits	Create content that encourages *brand preference and choice*	Create messages and experiences that reinforce the brand's benefits so as to enhance *brand satisfaction*	Create content that shows that customers are valued so as to encourage *repurchase/ brand loyalty*

As mentioned on page 164, touchpoints refer to all potential interactions between customers and your organization throughout the customer journey. Touchpoints can include advertising, social media, podcasts, blogs, demonstrations, testimonials, events, encounters with sales reps, websites, search engine results, mobile apps, social media posts, paid searches, display ads, sponsored posts, email newsletters, offline advertisements—television, billboard, radio, etc.—and in-person interactions at conferences, exhibitions, sales presentations, and other places.

Organizations don't always have complete control over all the customers' touchpoints (e.g., Tripadvisor reviews, mentioned in Exhibit 8.1), but they do have control over some. Organizations can also design the touchpoints that they do control so that (a) each reinforces the brand's benefits and that (b) each provides a seamless customer experience, such that customers are motivated to continue to the next stage of the journey with that brand under consideration. Negative experiences with the organization's product at various points along the customer journey deter customers from further considering that brand.

Finally, **content focus** refers to developing communications that best match the customers' place in their journey so that they receive the right content (i.e., communications), at the right time, in a way that establishes the brand's position, and are provided with the type of information they need at that stage. Content focus has implications for the communication objectives you set for the brand, such as brand name awareness and familiarity, enhancing brand knowledge, encouraging favorable brand attitudes (persuasion), choice, satisfaction, and brand repurchase/loyalty.

Why Map the Customer Journey?

By mapping this journey, organizations can envision the questions customers will likely ask along that journey, and thus the information they will need as they progress. Questions customers have at one stage in the journey may be quite different from those they have at a later stage. If you haven't mapped the customer journey, you probably haven't thought about your marketing communications from customers' perspectives. Moreover, you have probably not considered how all touchpoints need to communicate and reinforce the benefits promised from the brand and how all touchpoints motivate continuation along the journey. It's also likely that you have not considered how to design content at each stage. By explicitly mapping the customer journey, you gain a more complete and integrated view of what your touchpoints need to look like.

How to Map the Customer Journey

There are several ways to map the customer journey. You can do so via questionnaires, user testing, interviews, focus groups, etc. You can also use behavioral data, like Google Analytics or some custom analytics. You can speak with your customer service people to find out problems customers have, which can help you understand where they are in the customer journey. You can also reach out to companies that specialize in mapping customer

By explicitly mapping the customer journey, you gain a more complete and integrated view of what your touchpoints need to look like.

journeys. Finally, you can map the journey according to the standard stages explained in the following sections using the touchpoints from your analytics.

The Customer Journey Is Increasingly Online

These days, most of the customer journey takes place online. This fact isn't surprising for B2C brands, but it is becoming increasingly true for B2B brands as well. According to Forrester, 68 percent of the customer journey is completed anonymously, before a salesperson speaks with a prospect.[4] CSO Insights, the research division of Miller Heiman Group, says more than 70 percent of B2B prospects fully define their needs before engaging with a sales representative, and almost half identify specific solutions before reaching out.[5]

Touchpoints Are the Keys to Customer Delight

Organizations should focus on three things with touchpoints. First, is the same message being communicated by each touchpoint at that stage in the journey? Touchpoints need to be consistent and complementary in reinforcing the brand's purported benefits.

Second, does each touchpoint provide a positive customer experience that motivates them along the customer journey? If not, customers may abandon further consideration of your brand, wasting all the efforts you have engaged in previously.

Third, recall that customer delight is one barrier to competitive entry. Each touchpoint provides an opportunity to delight customers—providing not just what customers expect but also going beyond a positive experience and delighting them. Providing positive and delight-inducing experiences along the customer journey is also the goal known as CX (for "customer experience").

Exhibit 8.2 on page 176 illustrates an example, from a customer journey mapping company like Heart of the Customer, of a person named Jane looking for healthcare services.[6] Notice the problems Jane faces at different touchpoints along her journey. These are not good outcomes from the perspective of the customer journey.

TOUCHPOINTS THROUGHOUT THE CUSTOMER JOURNEY

It goes without saying that *the benefits in your positioning statement should be front and center of all touchpoints.* In addition, communication content should be clear and align with customers' questions at each stage of their journey along with elements of the message platform. In other words, consider what content you use to create brand awareness when customers search for information. If they are aware of your brand, what content is aligned with your brand benefits and gets your brand into customers' consideration set, and ultimately helps with the choice stage?

> ***The benefits in your positioning statement should be front and center of all touchpoints.***

Consumer psychologists and communications experts have outlined several important perspectives on what content characteristics can affect customers at different stages of the customer journey. A detailed presentation on all these perspectives is beyond the scope of this book, though we provide references to some of that material.[7] In Exhibit 8.3, on page 177, we present the major objectives for each step and provide some suggestions that should get you on your way.

EXHIBIT 8.2. Journey of a Specific Customer

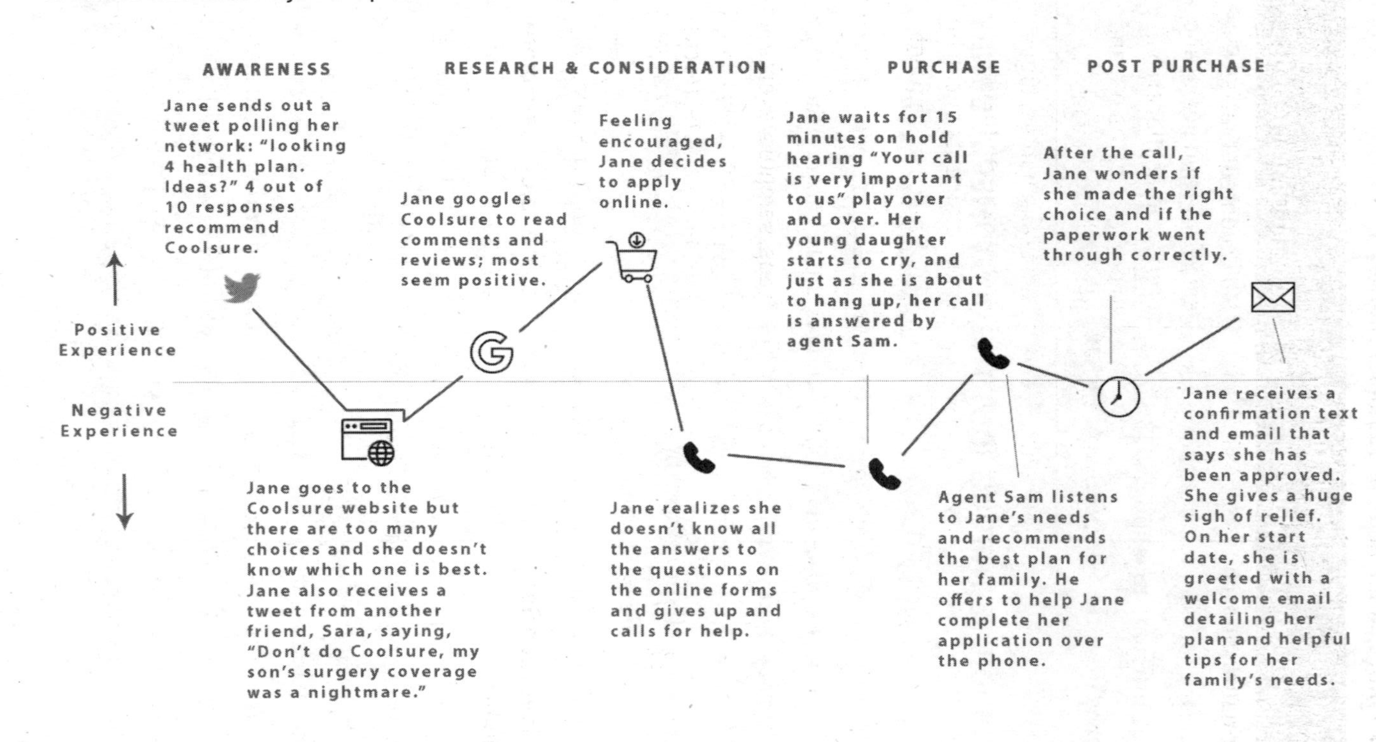

EXHIBIT 8.3. Content and the Customer Journey

Stage of the Customer Journey	Main Objective for Marketing	Content Characteristics
Information Search	Get Attention	Make content that is surprising and novel, and brand names that are easy to process, pleasant, and personally relevant
	Enhance Brand Familiarity	Use brand names, logos, and packaging that have visual elements or can be visualized; use frequent advertising; use social media, PR, influencers, and opinion leaders; use blogs, samples, events, out-of-home advertising (bus, taxi, vehicle, trucks), white papers; use search engine optimization; use promotional products
Consideration Set Formation	Enhance Brand Familiarity	Familiar brands are more likely to be considered
	Enhance Brand Inclusion in the Consideration Set	Use price- and nonprice-oriented promotions; use credible/expert/trustworthy endorsers; use information that supports/demonstrates brand benefits; compare the brand to the market leader in communications

Stage of the Customer Journey	Main Objective for Marketing	Content Characteristics
Choice	Enhance Brand Preference and Choice	See above. Promote positive user experiences/ reviews, particularly from similar others; promote brand's consistency with customer values
Experience/Usage	Ensure Positive Usage Experiences/ Satisfaction	Use frustration-free packaging; make usage instructions both visual and verbal; limit distractions during usage to allow consumers to focus on the brand experience; don't overpromise to avoid expectation disconfirmation; encourage savoring (for hedonic goods)
Repurchase	Foster Repurchase	Give something back to customers to reward past purchase (e.g., a free e-book, a discount for a future purchase, a free sample of another brand made by the organization, a thank-you card); use loyalty programs, quantity discounts; promote positive user experiences/ reviews

Brand Familiarity as a Starting Point

Since brand name familiarity plays a central role in the customer journey, let's look a bit deeper into this objective. **Brand name familiarity** (or brand awareness) refers to the extent to which customers recognize or can recall your brand name from memory. Creating brand name familiarity is essential for several reasons. First, consideration sets are often based on what brands customers recall from memory (e.g., "Where should we eat for dinner tonight?"). Unless your brand is highly memorable, it won't be considered.

Second, people tend to like and trust the brands they have heard of before. A brand with an unfamiliar name is likely to be scrutinized more than a well-known brand.

Third, recall that in chapter two, we described a brand as a set of associations customers link to the brand (its benefits, who uses it, how expensive it is, etc.). Customers will not have associations with brands they are unaware of. Brand name awareness is essential to creating a brand image (customers' perceptions or beliefs about the brand).

Finally, the brand name is one thing that links all pieces of content that organizations provide. Regardless of whether communications are in the form of white papers, email ads, exhibits, online displays, or blogs, the brand name is the one piece of information that links all these communications—including communication about your brand's benefits—under one "brand" roof.

Often, organizations enhance brand name awareness through frequent marketing communications; the logic is that greater exposure to the brand name helps make it more memorable. But because frequent advertising can be expensive, organizations need to think through other ways of enhancing brand name recall. Social media content (on sites like Pinterest, Twitter, Instagram, and TikTok) created by customers can be particularly powerful, since it reaches many individuals and at no cost to the organization.

Organizations can also opt for other mechanisms to establish brand name awareness, including the use of influencers and opinion leaders who can speak authoritatively and with credibility about the brand and its benefits. Organizations can also try to have the media feature their brand via the use of press releases or special events. A local art gallery with whom we have worked enhanced brand awareness using Google Maps, brand mentions in city tourist guides, and articles about art written by gallery members. Blogs as well as out-of-home advertising (which includes advertising on vehicles like buses, taxis, delivery vehicles, or cars driven by organization members) can be useful in reaching many customers. Of course, search engine optimization related to the brand's website enhances customers' abilities to see your brand name and learn something about its benefits. Promotional products such as free T-shirts, pens, flash drives, hats, or other merchandise with the brand name on it can enhance brand name awareness when these products are used publicly and seen by other customers.

Two essential elements that foster brand name recall are the brand name itself and the brand's logo. These elements are relatively stable markers of the brand, and most content that organizations provide includes both features. What makes them memorable?

Customers' abilities to recall a brand from memory depend on whether organizations represent the brand visually, verbally, or in auditory form.[8] The more modalities a brand name is expressed in, the more paths in memory are available to retrieve the brand name from memory.[9] Consider Aflac as an example. The brand name itself cannot be represented as a picture, because "Aflac" doesn't mean anything. But because Aflac has used its quacking duck in TV ads, most of us can literally "hear" the duck that quacks out the name. Using jingles that include the brand name also enhances brand name awareness, because the song provides an auditory cue that facilitates brand name recall.

The same principle holds for brand logos. Some logos (like those of Shell, Apple, Nike, and McDonald's) depict the brand in a pictorial logo. Other companies, like Coca-Cola, have a purely word-based logo. The most memorable logos represent the logo in pictures and words. Some (like the British Heart Foundation) explicitly design the logo to clarify the brand benefits.

Moving Customers Through the Journey

Another helpful set of practical tactics you can use to create content for the customer journey comes from the understanding that persuasion is at the heart of moving customers along the journey. In other words, how customers move though the stages depends on how much they are persuaded by the arguments made by your brand.

Social psychologist Robert Cialdini has identified the following factors that influence people in things like their choices.[10] Use one or more of these tactics throughout the customer journey:

- Reciprocity: Customers value equality and balance, and since you are asking something from the customer, they will value something given back to them—such as a free e-book, a discount for a future purchase, a free sample of another brand made by the organization, or even a thank-you letter for their business.
- Scarcity: Customers value rare objects more than common ones. Therefore, limited availability and exclusive memberships

persuade people to act sooner rather than later. We all remember how scarcity of toilet paper during the pandemic induced panic buying and purchase of brands at high prices. The same holds true when parents create in-store mayhem during the winter holiday season, fighting among themselves to land the toys their kids really want as gifts. Organizations can simulate scarcity through time-limited promotions (i.e., "25 percent off today only!").

- Authority: This principle focuses on the types of people providing the messages. People tend to listen to credible and knowledgeable experts, or anybody who is viewed as such, including athletes as well as doctors and scientists. At some level, we have already discussed opinion leaders in driving positive attitudes. But if two brands are equivalent in terms of attitudes, and one is endorsed by an authority figure, the one so endorsed will most likely be chosen. Speakers of authority are powerful in driving choice because, unlike your organization, they have no vested interest in whether people do or do not buy your brand.
- Commitment and Consistency: Customers want beliefs and behaviors to be consistent with their values and self-image. From a commitment standpoint, organizations can sometimes encourage choice and repeat purchase by developing commitment (or loyalty) programs, which give customers discounts or special deals given their loyalty to the organization. From a consistency perspective, customers will likely reward (by brand purchase) organizations whose principles and values are akin to their own. Sourcing products from earth-friendly suppliers

and using earth-friendly packaging, for example, have made for loyal customers of organizations like Patagonia. Consumer responsibility programs like that of Toms Shoes, which donates a pair of shoes to individuals in impoverished countries for every pair of shoes purchased, can also make brands stand out from others by virtue of their consistency with customers' values.

- Liking: Customers prefer to be with people they like. For this reason, likeable salespeople, customer service agents, repair specialists, etc. are more likely to encourage purchase when customers are choosing among brands with similar benefits.
- Consensus (or Social Proof): Customers tend to assume the actions of others are correct behavior they could emulate. This is why customer reviews and testimonials tend to work so well.

Who Does This Well? An Example

To see an example of an organization with consistent messaging and interactions throughout the customer journey, look no further than the Liberty Mutual insurance example in chapter four. Basically, Liberty Mutual is positioning around the two benefits of customization and a reasonable price. Their tagline is "Liberty Mutual customizes your insurance so you only pay for what you need." If you search online for insurance, you will find that the Google text on the search engine results page for Liberty Mutual itself says part of that tagline. Go to Liberty Mutual's website and the first thing you see is "Only Pay for What You Need." If you watch TV, you'll see ads for Liberty Mutual, and no matter the ad execution or content, the ads will all say, "Only Pay for What You Need." Go to Instagram, and Liberty Mutual's bio says, “We’re here to save people money with customized insurance.” Go to TikTok, and you’ll see the same messages.

There have been many different ads for this company, some very strange, but the company’s messaging consistency has significantly boosted their recall score.[11] Thus, they have achieved the brand familiarity we discussed before. The point is that *customers should see the same message regardless of the touchpoint along their journey.*

RECHECK YOUR POSITIONING

After you’ve positioned your product and made it come alive throughout the customer journey, you need to see if your activities resulted in a change in customers’ perceptions. Remember that positioning happens in the minds of customers in the market, so the best way to show success in positioning is through a perceptual map. Since the perceptual map you created in chapter two is a snapshot in time, we suggest you update the perceptual map every three to six months. This way you can see how well your activities have changed market perceptions. You also get an update on how your competitors are being viewed.

If your perceptual map shows no change, this could be due to competitor’s efforts (which is why we played out a competitive game in chapter five). In addition, you should check to make sure your messaging platform was followed. Finally, take another snapshot three months later to see if perceptions changed. Given how much informational clutter exists in our environment, it may take longer to see changes in market perceptions than you had anticipated.

SPEAK THE LANGUAGE OF BUSINESS

As Tricia Weener, EVP and chief marketing officer of KONE Corporation, puts it, "Speaking non-marketing, non-fluffy language [to the C suite] is what is important—and being able to be credible around the results that you're going to get." Weener is referring to the tendency for organizations to talk about concepts like "quality," "value," "strategy," "reputation," "position," and "branding"—while often, the president, CEO, CFO, and other members of the executive team are instead talking about "assets," "return on assets," "velocity," "leverage," and (if you work in a publicly owned company) "P/E multiple" and "firm value."

It's true that every business function has its own specialized vocabulary. But if marketing professionals from different parts of your company define marketing terms in different ways, you can count on creating confusion and skepticism in the minds of others in your company. In some ways, this problem is unique to marketing. Accounting and finance, for example, have standardized languages. "Net present value," "assets," "liabilities," and "cash flow statement," for example, are all terms that have standardized meanings. The definitions for accounting come from Generally Accepted Accounting Principles (also known as GAAP). Marketing does not have such principles.

Make a point of agreeing on marketing terms that you use every day. Creating a common marketing language introduces efficiency in your marketing meetings. Equally important, you generate coherent marketing strategies that everyone can understand *and* execute as intended. Finally, you will find it easier to translate the vocabulary of marketing into the language of business used by high-level executives in your company.

In short, translate your positioning activities into business language.[12] This is what will make your positioning credible not only to customers in the market, but also to the C-suite.

PLAYBOOK RULE #8

Align touchpoints to communicate benefits throughout the customer journey.

To sum up, executing on your positioning statement means *developing a message platform* that includes who you plan to target and with which benefits being central. Executing on the statement also means *mapping the customer journey* and *developing content* that reinforces the brand's positioning across all *touchpoints*. Content should reflect brand's *communication objectives*. The main action point for you, the reader, is to develop the message platform for your proposed positioning and outline the customer journey and touchpoints. Examine how you can use the touchpoints to consistently communicate the brand's benefits throughout the customer journey. Before moving on, let's summarize the main points.

KEY TAKEAWAYS

1. In order to execute on the positioning statement, you need to construct a message platform that includes (a) background information regarding the brand in its competitive context, (b) a description of the target segment(s) and who they are, (c) the positioning statement(s) (which indicates what target customers care about and the brand's associated benefits,

along with proof points that the brand can deliver on them), and finally (d) examples of compelling and awesome messages based on the positioning statement.

2. A key to executing on the message platform is to map the customer journey from the point where customers are first thinking about purchasing a brand to the point where they have purchased, experienced, and reflected on their brand purchase.
3. All touchpoints should align with each stage of the customer journey to reinforce the brand's benefits. In this way, the brand's benefits are synergistic in telling a compelling message about the brand's benefits to customers.
4. Making customers aware of your brand and making it familiar to them is critical. Without enhancing brand awareness and familiarity, customers will not continue with further stages of the journey.
5. Continue to gather perceptual data from the market, including target customers, and use this data to develop new perceptual maps. In this way, you are learning about your success in creating the brand perceptions noted in your positioning statement.
6. Use this data to convince members of the C-suite that your marketing efforts are effective.

GROW YOUR BRAND

Now that you have done the hard work of segmenting the market based on brand benefits, obtaining a perceptual map of you and the competitors in your market, developing a positioning statement that is credible and defensible, and executing it throughout the customer journey, your organization might consider new ways to grow.

DEVELOP A NEW BRAND?

One viable option for an organization to grow is to develop an entirely new brand targeted to a different segment of consumers who want other brand benefits. Or your organization might acquire an existing brand on the market and add it to your brand portfolio. Many organizations do one or both of these things. As discussed previously, Procter & Gamble's diaper category includes individual brands like Pampers, Luvs, All Good, and Charlie Banana. Marriott International has brands that include Ritz-Carlton, St. Regis, JW Marriott, W Hotels, Sheraton, Westin, and Le Méridien (among others).

Growth by developing a new individual brand can have some advantages. First, doing so makes sense if your organization sees new opportunities in other market segments where the original brand name would create unfortunate associations or confusion in potential customers' minds. For example, General Motors opted to create its Saturn brand at a time when their brands were not doing well. The new brand, with the tagline "A different kind of company; a different kind of car," signaled that Saturn was a far cry from what one expected from other General Motors products. Creating a new brand also insulates the organization's original brand if the new brand is a flop. Finally, creating a new brand makes sense if the organization plans to phase out the original brand.

On the other hand, developing a new brand can have downsides. First, it is more expensive to introduce a new brand, since your organization will need to go through all the steps described in previous chapters, but this time with the new brand in mind. Additionally, by developing a new brand, your organization will not be able to take advantage of the equity you have already invested in building the original brand. Specifically, the original brand is presumably familiar to customers, and brand name awareness has already been established. The organization has determined that the brand is aligned with the firm's strengths. The organization has already invested in research to understand the market for its original brand. It has invested time and money in messaging that communicates brand benefits, has enhanced brand choice, has enhanced brand usage experiences, and facilitated post-usage experiences. Presumably, some customers are loyal to the brand and will advocate on its behalf to others (through positive word of mouth online or offline). Such positive word-of-mouth communication is more credible than communication that comes from the organization. If your organization decides to introduce a new brand, these investments in the brand cannot be leveraged.

In this chapter we show how your organization can grow its *current* brand and leverage its equity. We identify three paths to brand growth: (1) growth through brand strength, (2) growth through brand extensions, and (3) growth through brand admiration.

PATH #1: GROWTH THROUGH BRAND STRENGTH

In chapter two, we showed that a strong brand provides numerous benefits to firms (see Exhibit 2.2 on page 43). Strong brands can keep out competitors by constructing barriers to entering their market. Strong brands can endure over time, enhance employee motivation and retention, and facilitate customers' brand loyalty and advocacy behaviors. Hence, one path to brand growth is to improve brand strength. Often, this approach emphasizes penetrating one's current market segment to become the market leader.

Ways to Make Brands Stronger

How can brands become stronger? In chapter two, we indicated that strong brands have positive, distinctive (i.e., unique), and highly salient (i.e., memorable) benefits. Hence, to grow through brand strength, the organization should (a) enhance how salient (top of mind) the current brand's benefits are to customers, (b) make the benefits they want more distinctive relative to competitors' brands benefits, and (c) enhance the extent to which the benefits are viewed as positive.

To illustrate, let's say that you are a car manufacturer targeting a segment that places high importance on safety (a functional benefit) and a smooth riding experience (an experiential benefit). Other brands on the market compete on things that different market segments regard as important (like "style," "reliability," or "status"). To date, you have done an excellent job of delivering on these benefits in the ways described in chapter eight. That is, your communications platform emphasizes these benefits, and you have successfully cultivated perceptions of these benefits throughout the customer journey.

Additionally, let's assume that you are competing directly with two other manufacturers who are also doing well in creating these same perceptions for their brands on safety and a smooth riding experience, as revealed by the perceptual map shown in Exhibit 9.1. These perceptions correspond with *Consumer Reports*, which gives your brand and the others you are competing against a score of 78 out of 100.

The question is this: How can you better compete with the other brands that are targeting the same customers that you are? How can you enhance the extent to which your brand offers *positive, distinctive,* or *salient benefits*? One option is to engage in more communications, spending lots of money to enhance how quickly customers have your brand come to mind. Doing so would strengthen the salience of your brand's benefits, but at an economic cost.

EXHIBIT 9.1

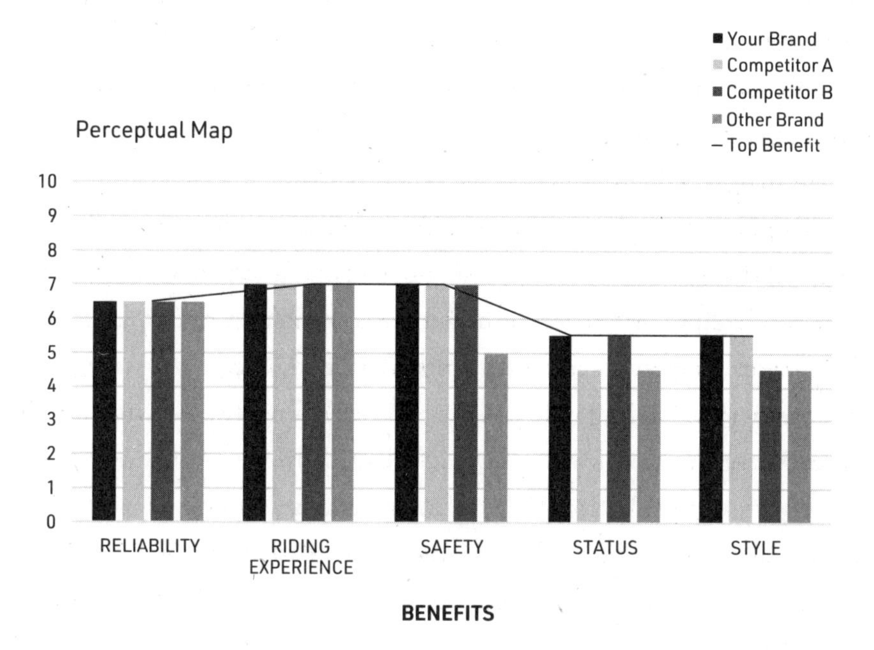

Many organizations focus on adding more features to make their brand more *distinctive* by adding new benefits, such as enhancing and emphasizing the brand's style as well as its safety and riding experience. Here, the brand would be distinctive relative to your direct competitors (who focus on safety and riding experience) because the benefit of style is not something that your competitors are emphasizing. Doing so would make sense if your target customers find the added benefit to be important. If they don't, your brand is distinctive but not necessarily more positive than other brands on what they do find important.

From our perspective, perhaps the best option is to see how you can enhance the level (i.e., positivity) of the benefit. We think this is a good strategy, because by enhancing the level of benefits your target customers find important, your brand also becomes more distinctive and salient. That is, to the extent that your brand outshines your competitors on the level of these benefits, your brand also becomes more distinctive in the eyes of target customers. It becomes distinctive not by providing something entirely different, but by being so much better than the brands it directly competes against. Because it is distinctive, customers are more likely to remember the brand name and its benefits, making the brand and its benefits more salient than before. Hence, by focusing on the positivity of your brand's benefits, you are also indirectly enhancing the other two drivers of brand strength (distinctiveness and salience).

How can you enhance the level of the benefits desired by your customers? In this instance, how can you improve customers' perceptions that your brand is safer and offers a smoother ride than your competitors? Perhaps your organization can invest in new proprietary technologies that enhance one or both benefits of the brand. Perhaps new features can be added (e.g., antilock brakes) or improved (e.g., better suspension) that up the level of the safety and smooth ride benefits (see Exhibit 1.1 on page 13 on how product features relate to benefits).

To illustrate how organizations can enhance the level of the benefit they offer, consider Dropbox. There were other cloud-based products on the market before Dropbox made its debut. For example, Xdrive, a service by AOL, offered five gigabytes of free storage.[1] But as the founder of Dropbox said about preexisting file storage software, "I tried everything I could find but each product inevitably suffered problems with Internet latency, large files, bugs, or just made me think too much."[2] So, the existing processes were highly cumbersome for customers.

Dropbox delivered a cloud-based solution, providing the benefit of "access from anywhere" and "collaboration" among multiple users.

Since then, Dropbox has enhanced the level of these functional benefits (making them more positive than before) while adding new functional benefits like security, productivity sharing, task management, and more. By upping the extent to which the brand offers a well-established benefit and adding new benefits that customers care about, Dropbox has grown by more deeply penetrating its existing market.

Benefits of Growth Through Brand Strength

Growing through brand strength is important, and for more reasons than just for market segment penetration. A strong brand is also attractive to other brands that want to partner with it through co-branding or brand alliances. With **co-branding**, two brands from separate organizations market a new brand together. Examples include Adidas Porsche Design athletic shoes, Dr Pepper and Bonne Bell lip balms, and Ford Harley-Davidson trucks. Co-branding allows each brand to grow, become more profitable, and enhance brand loyalty while also appealing to the same customer base. Ideally, the brands representing the co-branded product are highly popular and well regarded, making their match even more popular. Co-branding also works well when each brand is known for its benefits, but their combined benefits make the new co-branded options highly desirable (consider, for example, Good Humor Oreo Cookies & Creme ice cream).

A strong brand is also attractive to other brands that want to partner with it through co-branding or brand alliances.

A **brand alliance** is a partnership between two brands with common strategic goals. Consider, for example, the alliance between BMW and Louis Vuitton. These two brands were natural partners, given their shared focus on the benefits of status and luxury. When BMW launched its BMW i8 sports model, Louis Vuitton exclusively designed and crafted a four-piece set of suitcases and bags that matched the car's interior and fit perfectly in the back of the vehicle. Or consider the alliance between Uber and Spotify. With this alliance, Uber riders can play their own music, making the Uber ride feel more personalized. In addition, Uber riders may become more likely to subscribe to Spotify Premium so they can listen to the music they like inside and outside of Uber rides. Each brand benefits. Uber benefits because its competitors, like Lyft, do not offer similar services. Spotify benefits because the Uber experience underscores Spotify's ability to provide personalized music (an experiential benefit).

So, once you have a strong brand, you can grow it even more by linking the benefits of your brand with the benefits of an alliance partner, further enhancing customer delight and growth prospects.

PATH #2: GROWTH THROUGH BRAND EXTENSIONS

A second path to brand growth is through brand extensions.[3] **Brand extensions** leverage your brand name by using it in a different product category.[4]

Examples of Brand Extensions

For example, Gatorade sports drink has recently extended its brand to the gummy immune support product category.[5] Arm & Hammer originated in 1846 as a baking soda product, but the brand's deodorizing benefit allowed it to extend into myriad products for which deodorizing is essential. Representative Arm & Hammer products today include kitty litter, car air fresheners, changing pads, air purifiers, diaper bags and pails, carpet cleaners, toothpaste, body wash, foot care products, and more. Additionally, as mentioned previously, the deodorizing benefit has allowed alliances with other brands, including Dutch Boy interior paint and Hefty trash bags. In short, being a brand known for a particular benefit enables growth opportunities in other domains where the brand's benefits are relevant.

As another example, Ivory was initially introduced to the market as a brand of soap known for the benefits of cleanliness and softness to the skin. These well-established benefits put Ivory in an excellent position to extend the Ivory name to new product categories where cleanliness and softness are desirable benefits for consumers. With that in mind, Ivory extended the brand to Ivory shampoo, Ivory conditioner soap, Ivory laundry detergent, and Ivory deodorant.[6] Similarly, the name Honda originally referred only to the motorcycles that used its motors. However, Honda has since extended this name to automobiles and brands like Honda Powersports, Honda Aircraft, Honda Marine, and Honda Power Products. Since the brand name (Ivory/Honda) was being extended to a product category that the brand had not previously competed in, the brand extension created a new path to growth. The FedEx brands we discussed in chapter five represent another example of brand extensions.

Being a brand known for a particular benefit enables growth opportunities in other domains where the brand's benefits are relevant.

Extension branding is not just for product brands. They are highly relevant to entertainment and celebrity brands too. Consider Disney, whose family-friendly films, cruise line, cable channel, hotels, theme parks (Disneyland, Disney World), resorts, and live shows (like Disney on Ice) each reinforce the meaning of Disney as an organization that captivates the imagination of kids and adults alike. Consider celebrities like Oprah, whose relatability, initially established through her talk show, has been extended to her film roles, book club, and magazine. Jennifer Lopez's beauty has made her a natural not only for movie and music roles but also for her fragrance, makeup, and skincare lines. Similarly, Martha Stewart, who originally started in restoring and decorating homes, has become synonymous with "home" in light of her decorating books, *Martha Stewart Living* magazine, retail products, media channel (Martha Stewart Living Omnimedia), and TV show.

Benefits of Brand Extensions

Brand extensions offer several benefits to marketers.[7] First, it can be easier and less costly for marketers to develop brand extensions, because the brand name is already known to customers (i.e., brand awareness is high). Customers will also have some knowledge about the brand, which allows them to infer what benefits the brand extension will have. Additionally, customers may believe that the extension will credibly deliver on the benefits of the brand extension, because the brand is already known for credibly providing them in the form of the original brand.

Another advantage is that by having several offerings associated with the same brand, the brand's meaning becomes more expansive, as customers now associate multiple offerings with the brand name, not just one. For example, Gerber means not just baby food but all types of baby care. Patagonia means not just climbing gear but all manner of sustainably sourced outdoor clothing and equipment. Whereas Nike originally stood for well-designed running shoes, the brand is now synonymous with sports apparel and a casual-living lifestyle. Likewise, FedEx, first known for its fast shipping, now is known as a service that supports individuals and businesses with benefits of ease of use and one-stop shopping and service (their specific features include shipping, printing, shredding, direct mail, laminating, notarizing, expediting passports, and more).

Extension branding works best when the benefits of the original product are desirable and important in the extension category. If they aren't, and if the company is looking for new growth opportunities, they should use a different name on the new product. Bic, which is known for inexpensive plastic items (lighters, pens, disposable razors), extended the Bic name to perfume. The product was a flop because customers inferred that the perfume would come in plastic bottles, be cheap, or perhaps smell like lighter fluid (associations linked with other Bic products).

Brand Extension Downsides and Remedies

A potential downside to brand extensions is that if the new brand gains negative support from the marketplace because it performs poorly, or is subject to a brand scandal, the negative feelings about the brand extension could hurt the other offerings marketed under the brand name. One way to avoid this situation is to use an endorsement brand strategy. With an **endorsement brand**, the original brand supports (or "endorses") the new brand, creating a bit of psychological distance between the original brand and the brand it endorses. For example, Marriott introduced Courtyard by Marriott, using the well-known Marriott name to endorse the new lower-priced hotel. By being the endorser, Marriott was able to leverage its name as an excellent hotel for upscale travelers to introduce another superb hotel—this one for the less well-off traveler. Other examples of endorser brands include Polo by Ralph Lauren and Solar Turbines, advertised as "A Caterpillar Company." If you are developing a new brand that involves endorsement branding, or if you are responsible for a brand that uses this approach, the parent brand provides credibility and legitimacy to your new brand by virtue of its public support of the new offering, while simultaneously allowing your new brand to operate independently of the parent. If your brand fails, the parent brand will not be hurt as badly, because the parent merely "endorsed" your brand, not directed it.

A final downside of brand extensions is that sometimes brands can be extended to so many different product categories that the brand's meaning becomes unclear. For example, the Sony name is used on its PlayStation games, music, imaging and sensing products, financial services, consumer electronics, artificial intelligence, and more. With so many products having the Sony name, it is difficult for customers to know what benefits Sony stands for. The same can be said for Virgin, which made its debut as a retailer of recorded music (albums, CDs, etc.). Today, the Virgin name has been extended to other forms of entertainment (books, games, casinos, radios), experiences (airlines, space travel), health and wellness, money, and financing of start-ups. Having so many brand extensions can enhance brand name awareness. However, too many extensions whose benefits are only loosely connected to one another can diffuse the brand's image.

PATH #3: GROWTH THROUGH BRAND ADMIRATION

Recent research indicates a third and powerful path to growth; namely, attempting to make one's brand admired. Notably, this last path to growth builds on the previously mentioned paths.[8]

Before getting into the specifics of this path to growth, stop and think for yourself about brands you love, are attached to, or admire, or those to which you have a deep connection. This could be a product, a service, a company, an experience, or any other type of brand listed in Exhibit 2.1 (on page 40). You might have such a strong personal connection to the brand you are attached to that you would feel great distress were the brand to be taken off the market. In fact, the more the brand matters to you and relates to your life, the more difficult it would be to imagine what it would be like to live without the brand.

Like most people who are attached to a brand, you are probably highly motivated to not just buy the brand repeatedly, but to perform other behaviors that help the brand. For example, you are more likely to refuse to buy a competitor's brand if your preferred brand is unavailable. You are more likely to advocate on behalf of the brand, pay more to obtain it, defend the brand if others speak negatively about it, and pay a price premium for the brand.

That people connect with certain brands in this deep and profound way is obvious. Consider how attached people are to their iPhones. Witness the long lines of cars at a Chick-fil-A. Watch the excitement of people seeing their favorite movie star or the fervor of fans watching their favorite sports team or political candidate. Wouldn't it be wonderful if your brand had similar reactions from your customers? For the purposes of our book, we will call brands that create such devotion by customers "admired brands." You could easily see how this would be a path to growth. How do organizations get customers to be so devoted?

It turns out that brands that customers are attached to in this deep and profound way have three characteristics: they resonate with (are closely related to) the self, because they are brands that customers trust, love, and respect given the functional (enabling), experiential (enticing), and symbolic (enriching) benefits that the brand provides.[9]

Characteristics of Admired Brands

According to researchers, customers admire those brands that they trust, love, *and* respect.[10] **Brand trust** is the degree to which the brand can be counted on to deliver functional benefits when customers need them. Brand trust is earned over time as customers encounter the brand repeatedly. Through repeated brand encounters, customers learn that they can depend on the brand to be there for them and to have their best interests at heart.

Beyond providing high levels of trust, customers also love admired brands because they make them feel good in light of their experiential benefits. **Brand love** is the degree to which customers have a strong degree of affection for the brand. They adore it and want it to be part of their lives because of how much it pleases them. Customers love those brands that gratify them.

Admired brands are also respected by customers given the symbolic brands they provide. **Brand respect** is the degree to which customers look up to the brand and hold it in high esteem. Customers respect brands that do what is morally right, even if it comes at a cost to the brand. They respect the brand for what it stands for and how it speaks to important human values (like universalism). They regard the brand as aspirational, because it speaks to higher-order human values.

Whereas trust, love, and respect alone can positively affect brand purchase, enduring *commitment* to a brand is greatest when brands evoke all three. We can understand why this is true when we look at human relationships. To illustrate, a marital relationship is strongest when both parties love, trust, and respect each other. Loving one's partner without trusting them leads to an anxiety-ridden relationship that will never last. Trusting one's partner without loving them results in a cold and unfulfilling relationship. Loving one's partner without respecting them leads to relationship instability. The same is true for relationships characterized by trust but not involving respect. The longest and most enduring committed relationships are characterized by love, trust, *and* respect.[11]

Let's apply these ideas to brands, using Caterpillar and Patagonia as B2B and B2C examples, respectively. Caterpillar's heavy-duty machinery, combined with its efficient supply chain, provide functional benefits that enable customers (dealers) to get the most challenging construction jobs done. In addition, they ensure that urgently needed specialty parts ship to local dealers in the shortest time possible. Dealers are concerned about the future of their businesses once they retire, especially since many of their companies are family owned. To address this concern, Caterpillar organizes conferences and networking events that introduce dealers' children to Caterpillar and get them excited about the company (experiential and symbolic benefits). This activity of Caterpillar warms the hearts of its dealers. As members of the Caterpillar community, dealers believe they are doing good things for the world (because its mission is to make, sell, and tend to machines that make the world work). This belief gives dealers a sense of pride, and sends a powerful signal to others about who they are and what they do. Pride and identity signaling are symbolic and enriching benefits that Caterpillar dealers care about.

Patagonia's functional benefits empower its customers to overcome common outdoor sports challenges. It offers apparel and hard goods that perform in any weather condition: rain, heat, wind, or freezing temperatures. Patagonia's products entice customers: the clothing is soft and gentle to the skin, the bags and backpacks are comfortable, and the product designs are appealing (experiential benefits). Most important, Patagonia does an excellent job at providing symbolic benefits, offering hope for the future, and indeed for humankind, by being a leader in addressing climate change through sustainably sourced and ecologically minded product ingredients.

Brand Admiration and Brand Strength

It's important to note that to enhance brand admiration, brands must provide functional, experiential, and symbolic benefits, and strong levels of these desired benefits. Specifically, the most admired brands offer functional benefits that empower customers, experiential benefits that entice them, *and* symbolic benefits that enrich them. Doing so consistently over time enhances brand admiration, because the brands become trusted, loved, *and* respected brand relationship partners.

The most admired brands offer functional benefits that empower customers, experiential benefits that entice them, and symbolic benefits that enrich them.

In short, to become admired, a brand needs to exhibit brand strength on each benefit type. Having a strong brand that is widely recognized as providing high levels of one particular benefit is not enough to build brand admiration. Instead, the brand needs to be strong on all three benefit types.[12]

Brand Admiration and Brand Extensions/Alliances

Building an admired brand is an important path to growth, as brands can grow among a core set of brand users by becoming trusted, loved, and respected because of the benefits they offer. However, admired brands provide other paths to growth too, since customers are highly likely to accept extensions to the brands they trust, love, and respect. Additionally, admired brands are more likely to be recruited by other brands as brand partners in a brand alliance or co-branding opportunity. Hence, the brand admiration framework encapsulates and subsumes the previously mentioned paths to growth. A critical practical advantage of the brand admiration framework is that it builds in not only the notion of strength from brand benefits but also brand strength from the standpoint of customer-brand relationships.

More on Brand Admiration

We encourage readers to examine C. Whan Park, Deborah J. MacInnis, and Andreas B. Eisingerich's 2016 book, *Brand Admiration*. In it, they provide an expansive perspective on the science behind the concept of brand admiration, how employees within an organization can build brand admiration, the relationship between brand admiration and a company's mission statement, how admired brands can be strengthened and leveraged, how admired brands add value to customers and companies, and how to build a brand admiration dashboard. As they explain, admired brands offer numerous benefits to organizations. They (1) enhance revenue, (2) reduce costs, (3) facilitate further growth through brand extensions, (4) help to recruit and retain organizational talent, (5) boost morale among the organization's employees, (6) provide second chances to organizational mishaps, (7) protect the brand from new market entrants, (8) facilitate alliances with other admired brands, and (9) enhance the brand's marketplace value. Each of these outcomes is of direct value to individuals who occupy C-suite positions within the organization.

Brand Admiration Is Possible for Every Organization

If you are in a B2B context, it's likely you are thinking that brand admiration applies only to consumer brands. It's true that it's easier for consumer brands, since they often are based on symbolic and experiential benefits. But if you were the first in your industry to provide all three benefits, you would be way ahead of all your competitors. Today, B2B brands do a good job at providing functional benefits, but many fail to consider how to build in experiential and symbolic benefits. A recent study by Deloitte Deutschland identified various ways that brands can build excitement (an experiential benefit) into their brands, such as by creating surprise or delight. And B2B brands can provide symbolic benefits by highlighting their strong reputation and respect in the marketplace, by creating special status among certain customer groups, or by appealing to values like supporting the earth that customers are likely to find important too.

As brands, celebrities are known for their experiential benefits, but they can provide functional benefits too, such as their versatility in the roles they play or providing information on how they addressed a challenging personal issue. They can also provide symbolic benefits such as supporting the welfare of vulnerable people or supporting efforts to rehabilitate the environment.

Nonprofits typically provide symbolic benefits by showcasing how donations can help others. But they can also provide functional benefits such as showcasing how donations reduce others' pain or fear, or making it highly convenient for people to make donations. And they can provide experiential benefits such as providing heartwarming letters to donors about the people they have helped.

Interestingly, organizations can use customer data to determine the extent to which their brand offers stronger levels of functional, experiential, and symbolic brand benefits than their competitors do, and the extent to which it is trusted, loved, and respected. The competitive standing of the brand on these benefits and relationship drivers provides crucial diagnostic information to organizations on how they can build brand admiration further.

PLAYBOOK RULE #9

A focus on the benefits reveals more ways to grow your organization.

It is clear that focusing on customer benefits has many advantages for your organization. The main action point for you, the reader, is to consider the various paths to growing your brand and to assess the viability of each path now and over time. Before moving on, let's summarize the main points of chapter nine.

KEY TAKEAWAYS

1. Organizations can grow by developing new brands. However, this path to growth is expensive from the standpoint of time and money and does not leverage the equity that the organization has built in developing their original brand. Instead, we advocate that brands look for growth opportunities from their existing brand.
2. One path to growth is by enhancing brand strength. This path involves upping the level of the brand's benefits such that they are greater (more positive and hence salient and distinctive) than what competitors offer. By enhancing brand strength, the organization is in a better position to penetrate the market more fully and take share away from competitors. Brand strength also enhances the brand's potential for co-branding and alliances with other brands.
3. A second path to growth is through brand extensions: using the same brand name on a product in a different category. This path leverages the existing meaning of the brand and its benefits, allowing customers to infer what the new product will be like as well as expanding the meaning of the brand. Extension branding is more cost-efficient than introducing an entirely different brand; however, a brand scandal can leave the brand franchise in a vulnerable position. An endorsement branding strategy can mitigate this problem to a certain extent.

4. A final path to growth is to enhance the extent to which the brand is admired. This can be accomplished by providing functional, experiential, *and* symbolic benefits so as to facilitate the three drivers of admired brands: trust, love, and respect. Admired brands offer numerous advantages to organizations, including financial ones. These organizational benefits are highly relevant to individuals who occupy C-suite positions within the organization.

FINAL WORDS

Our book is unique in providing an integrated, benefits-oriented perspective to benefit segmentation and target segment selection and brand positioning, as well as stress tests related to the credibility and defensibility of the benefits in the positioning statement. Additionally, it covers acting on the proposed positioning throughout the customer journey, and pursuing paths to growth. However, our focus on customer benefits is not new. It was the gifted marketing thinker Ted Levitt who originated the insight that customers want benefits. As we quoted earlier in the book, he famously quipped, "People don't want to buy a quarter-inch drill; they want a quarter-inch hole." He applied this idea to explain why industries disappeared and organizations failed.[1]

Levitt wrote about this in 1960. At first, we had thought that this was old news, and that modern organizations already thought this way about their markets, especially since it was such a straightforward, customer-focused perspective. Indeed, many people have heard the quip about a quarter-inch hole and think it's a cute idea. But instead, we found that this is not the way most organizations think. We hope that the playbook we provide here can cause more organizations to view their market and offerings differently.

We also hope that providing many reasons to think about customer benefits will encourage organizations to shift perspectives. For example, as Exhibit 1.3 emphasizes, a benefits focus helps organizations and guides marketing decision-making. We have also clarified how this focus provides an integrated perspective on previously disintegrated ideas, like market segmentation, target segment selection, positioning, company and competitor analysis, and marketing execution throughout the customer journey. Furthermore, we showed how a focus on benefits reveals new paths to growth.

We believe that organizations really want to serve their customers and have an inherent desire to be customer focused. The best way to really focus on customers is by focusing on the benefits they seek.

APPENDIX A

HOW TO IDENTIFY BENEFITS OF AN EXISTING BRAND

How can you identify the benefits that customers in your market want? The answer depends on whether you are trying to find a market for your product or whether you compete in an existing category.

Finding a New Market for an Existing Brand

This is a common approach for technology-focused products or start-ups. Typically, this approach involves first focusing on the features of the brand and what benefits your features provide, then asking which markets will want these benefits.

Here is an example. Google Glass was launched worldwide in May 2014. This was an optical head-mounted display, with approximately the same shape as a pair of normal eyeglasses. Its advanced features brought to life directions, emails, weather forecasts, a personalized contact list and, more important, offered the benefit of information accessibility. In a sense, it was the first iteration of augmented reality glasses targeted to the general consumer market.

The first version of the glasses, called the Explorer Edition, was on the market for a short time and then discontinued in January 2015. Observers and critics pointed to privacy concerns, a high price ($1,500), and a clunky design as the reason for the demise of the product.

But what else could Google do with these glasses, given the benefits the glasses provide?

Google found another market that needed these benefits: people in factories and other work environments who need the benefits of readily accessible information, hands-free work, and the ability to collaborate with others while on the job. However, finding a new market or category is not positioning; it's simply identifying a new market. As Google discovered after entering this new market, they had competition from Microsoft HoloLens and needed to position their product relative to the HoloLens.

Try this for yourself. Look at the features or characteristics of your own brand, whether it's an organization, business unit, product, service, start-up, experience, person, nonprofit, or place. Then connect those features or characteristics to customer benefits. Using the benefits, now think about customers in various markets where those benefits are desired.

Competing in an Existing Market

Alternatively, if you compete in an existing market, start with this market and take a customer's perspective. What benefits do customers in the market think about when considering one product versus others? There are a few ways to identify what benefits customers in an existing market find important.

Observe customers in real usage situations. Observational studies can be highly useful in seeing where customers get frustrated, upset, angry, disappointed, confused, or have other negative feelings from the use of a product or service. Observational study was among the various research techniques that revealed why cup holders in cars are so important to consumers. All else being equal, the nature, presence, and shape of cup holders can determine whether customers will consider a certain car. Why? They want the convenience of having their drink, their change, their sunglasses, etc., at their fingertips when driving.

Listen to customers. Yes, even unhappy ones. Focus groups and social media can be helpful in this regard. But pay attention to the benefits customers seek (not the features they want). To listen with social media, you can use services like Hootsuite, which allow you to listen for posts that include keywords, like your brand name. You can have it alert you at specific times, or you can have someone monitor it.

Use laddering. Laddering is a method of interviewing customers to determine the benefits they consider when making judgments and decisions. The primary goal of laddering is to identify what attributes of a product customers find important and then link these essential attributes to the benefits that drive customers' decisions. Here's a quick guide to laddering:

› ***Step 1: Find Differences Among Brands.*** Laddering is done individually, with one interviewer working with one respondent. It's not nearly as efficient a tool for data collection as focus groups are; however, the insights may be worth the effort. The interviewer first presents the respondent with a list of brands in the same category (e.g., Budweiser, Miller Lite, Heineken, and Corona). The respondent's job is to tell the interviewer how these brands differ in their attributes. Sometimes this job is made easier by presenting respondents with two brands and asking them to indicate how they are similar and how they are different. Sometimes it's made easier by asking respondents to consider other occasions in which they might use each brand, and what it is about each that makes it appropriate for that situation. No matter which method you use, the key is identifying the attributes that differentiate brands.

Typically, respondents can name only about ten to twelve attributes that distinguish brands in the category. If respondents don't know a lot about brands in the product category, it is useful to ask them which brand they use and what they like about it.

› ***Step 2: Identify Important Attributes.*** If you've successfully identified several features, ask the respondent which are most important in deciding which brand to buy in the category. Ranking the importance of features provides input to the next step: building the ladder.

› ***Step 3: Build a Ladder.*** The interviewer then tries to determine the consequences that the customers feel they experience from the product having a particular attribute. For example, the interviewer might say, "So, you've told me that the carbonation level of beers is important to you and that you like beers with lots of carbonation. Can you tell me what's so good about having carbonation?" The respondent answers with an outcome or benefit from having that attribute. Perhaps the outcome is that "lots of carbonation means that I feel full more quickly." The interviewer then "climbs the ladder" to find out why feeling full

> quickly is essential or desirable. The respondent may reply that she drinks less when she is full. When asked why drinking less is important, our customer may answer that she can avoid getting drunk if she drinks less. When asked why this outcome is important, the respondent may indicate that she likes to stay in control. Here, we see that the attribute of carbonation is linked to the critical benefit of "feeling full," which is ultimately linked to a need to "stay in control," which is a functional motivation.
>
> Let's take another customer who identifies a different attribute—expensiveness. He likes to drink premium, top-of-the-line beers. When asked what this brings him, he might reply that it gives him a superior product. When asked why this is important, he may reply that quality products convey a sophisticated image to people. When asked why this outcome is necessary, our customer may reply that he wants to impress others. When asked why he wants to impress others, it may become apparent that he has a strong need for boosting self-esteem or a strong need for belonging, which are symbolic motivations. In general, laddering leads customers from (1) attributes of a product to (2) the consequences of having these attributes to (3) the benefit with which their presence is associated.

If you focus your attention on benefits rather than product features, characteristics, and attributes, you will point your organization toward new products and services that solve customers' *real* problems. The result is likely to be more customers and greater revenues.

APPENDIX B

IDENTIFYING BENEFITS IN NEW PRODUCTS

You can also identify which benefits most resonate with customers regarding new products, as laddering works best with existing products. (If you are referring to a new-to-the-world type of product, read appendix C.) One way of identifying benefits is through experimentation. Specifically, you can provide potential customers with descriptions of products that have different benefits and see which resonate most.

Conjoint analysis is a technique that helps with this process. Conjoint analysis is a statistical technique that measures the relative importance customers place on various features or benefits. Conjoint analysis has many applications, one of which involves testing new product ideas. To use conjoint analysis to find benefits in new product ideas, researchers provide customers with hypothetical brands that vary in which benefits they provide and in the extent to which they provide these benefits. The conjoint analysis process involves presenting all the different combinations of features to a random selection of customers. This method takes the data and outputs the most important features associated with the various benefits. By examining customers' preferences for certain product concepts, you can evaluate which new product ideas are most popular and assess the importance of certain benefits relative to others.[1]

Marriott used the conjoint analysis approach to develop and implement a new hotel concept designed specifically for frequent business travelers, called Courtyard by Marriott.[2] The technique involved sorting features of a hotel into seven groups of benefits. An example is the benefit of leisure, which can be supported by the features of a sauna, exercise room, tennis courts, game rooms, etc. Another benefit is the convenience of eating at the hotel, which is supported by the features of a restaurant in the hotel or nearby, or room service. Conjoint analysis was also used to design the physical layout and services that Marriott provided.

Today, Courtyard has the largest global market share within Marriott's portfolio.[3] The effectiveness of using conjoint analysis changed the organization's approach to new product development, not just for Courtyard by Marriott but for many of Marriott's other hotel brands.

APPENDIX C

NEW-TO-THE-WORLD PRODUCTS

What should you be aware of when you are launching a new brand into a "new to the world" product category? Automobiles, airplanes, electricity, computers, e-books, and online gambling are all examples of "new to the world" products, meaning that such innovations did not exist before a certain time in history. When marketing a new-to-the-world product category, customers have to make a decision as to whether to stay with what they do already (i.e., traveling by horse and buggy, gaming at casinos) or move forward and buy the innovation. In short, users have something that works well enough and may not see a need to switch. As such, competitors in the old product category (horse and buggy carriers, casinos) are "do-nothing" competitors, meaning they don't see the need to do anything different.

We've seen companies who compete against the do-nothing competitor because they try to convince users that their product is simply better. Such was the case with e-books and Google Glass when they first came on the market. In these cases, understanding the benefits that customers want is essential to success.

There are many reasons why possible adopters of these products are hesitant. You should think of these reasons generally as reflecting a status quo bias; that is, forces that keep potential adopters with the status quo even when the benefits of changing outweigh the status quo. These forces slow down the rate of diffusion, which refers to how quickly the market will adopt your new product.

Everett Rogers wrote about this problem in his classic 1962 book *Diffusion of Innovations.*[4] Rogers focused on why some innovations diffuse quickly, while others do so slowly. His work has been applied to myriad disciplines, including technology, communications, and marketing. Rogers identified five characteristics of innovations that aid the diffusion of new ideas and products—many of which are essentially benefits that ease the risk of adoption.

1. **Relative Advantage** means that customers regard your innovation as demonstrably better than what customers are using now. This is necessary but not sufficient for increasing your product's adoption rate. If you have an innovation, make sure that customers are convinced that what you offer is superior to what they are buying now.
2. **Trialability** is the ability for customers to try out your innovation without purchasing it. Trialability is easy for products that give people a trial period. For example, Dropbox gives users two gigabytes of storage to help them try out the service. If you have an innovation, consider how you can give users a chance to evaluate it without purchasing anything.
3. **Ease of Use** refers to how intuitive and seamless it is for customers to use the innovation—even for the first time. A good

way to evaluate ease of use is to ask current customers (do not rely on people in your company, who will likely think it's already easy to use). Get a usability expert to help you. If your product is not easy to use, put enhancing ease of use on your action list.

4. **Observability** means that users can see the benefits of the product or service for themselves. Think of it this way: "You say your product provides these benefits, but how do I know I actually got these benefits?" Once, we worked with a machine protection company dealing with the status quo problem. The product was terrific, you could try it out, and it was easy to use. But when we asked the people at the company whether users could actually see that they were protected, they said not really. Given this problem, they began to work on a dashboard so people could *see* the benefit of protection.
5. **Compatibility**—perhaps the most significant factor influencing new product adoption and diffusion—means that the product works with the way we already do things. Let us illustrate this concept with an example. Over twenty years ago, Allen wrote a column for a popular technology website when e-book readers first came out. Using the benefits noted above, Allen mentioned that diffusion would take time. One reader disputed his suggestion, saying, "Today, more technologies are being developed that will facilitate the mass acceptance of e-books. A new generation of PDAs, cell phones, laptop computers, and flat-panel displays will make the efficient distribution of reading material an absolute pleasure. And your argument that books are to be 'treasured' as a personal symbol is ludicrous."

But Allen's point was that e-books were not compatible with how people read books. Indeed, these days e-books still sell less than regular books.[5]

Another example is Google Glass, which we discussed earlier. Allen was asked a few years ago about his prediction on the adoption of these glasses. Again, focusing on compatibility, he predicted that adoption would be very slow. As we mentioned, in 2017, Google stated that they planned to focus on factories and warehouses rather than the general market. Google Glass was not compatible with how the general public wore glasses but was very highly compatible with the fact that people who work in factories already wore goggles.

Don't neglect consideration of these benefits when you have a new-to-the-world product or are facing a market that is hesitant to purchase in your category.

APPENDIX D

BIG DATA AND CUSTOMER INSIGHTS

We write this book in a world consumed with "big data." Indeed, drawing insights from big data is one of the significant interests of marketers.[6] If you work in a company with teams—often called customer insight or data analytics teams—that are devoted to using data to segment the market, you might use such data for purposes of market segmentation. As Forrester says, "CI [customer insights] pros' interest in getting segmentation right remains quite high."

Yet some teams find it difficult to provide customer insights for big data. For example, big data might obtain behavioral data from customers' mobile phone records. Using a k-means clustering algorithm, anyone can undoubtedly find three clusters of customers and call them customer segments. But you will have no idea what benefits the customers who are in those clusters want. In other words, big data can be a blunt tool. When data is just too big, it isn't useful, because it doesn't tell you about your consumer's purchase behavior.[7] Profound insights are not possible, because you have no data about customers who bought your competitors' products or how the market views your products versus those of your competitors in terms of their benefits. As we stated in chapter one, this approach can lead to marketing myopia and puts organizations at a strategic disadvantage.

The operative word through all these efforts is "customer insight." Big data approaches likely will not provide insight into how customers might behave in the future, since they are based only on present-day behaviors. Forrester believes the future is in artificial intelligence segmentation,[8] which, because the data will be restricted to behaviors of customers you have data on, will keep you from seeing the entire market. Having data on your current customers does not reflect the total market. But benefits and customers' beliefs about brands and how they are different are central to understanding why people behave the way they do.

Instead, customer insight (CI) teams can get segmentation right by segmenting the market using the methods we have discussed. First, obtain the benefits that customers in your market want. (We discussed several ways to obtain benefits in appendix A.) Second, get a random sample from the market. Construct a survey instrument that includes the benefits that you believe customers in the market are looking for. Use a 100-point scale and ask customers to allocate those 100 points to those benefits that are most important to them (more points = greater importance). The number of respondents needed for this is much less than the typical amount of data required by your CI teams. This is because you need a random sample of customers in the market to get data for a customer survey, while you tend to need hundreds of thousands (if not more) data points just to train machine learning algorithms. You'll be using this data to segment the market using one of the approaches we described in chapter three (cluster analysis, focus groups, managerial judgment).

Along with benefits data from each respondent, tell your CI team to get the behaviors, traits, or any other data currently being gathered by the CI teams for these respondents. Next, use descriptors to characterize who is in each segment. Use discriminant analysis to see how these behaviors, traits, or other data relate to the benefit segments. Discriminant analysis seeks to find a linear combination of the behaviors, traits, etc., that separates the benefit segments. Discriminant analysis will give you the insights you need to understand the descriptive characteristics of each segment.

You can then conduct another study that queries customers on their perceptions of the various brands on the market regarding the benefits they seek. You can use this data to develop a perceptual map, as we describe in chapter two.

ACKNOWLEDGMENTS

We deeply appreciate Cynthia A. Zigmund for her help in crafting our book proposal, Matt Holt for having enough faith in us to publish this book, Katie Dickman for her guidance and helpful comments, Leah Baxter for her excellent editing, and our endorsers and colleagues for their support.

NOTES

Play #1: Focus on Benefits

1. C. Whan Park, Deborah J. MacInnis, and Andreas B. Eisingerich, *Brand Admiration: Building a Business People Love* (Hoboken, NJ: John Wiley & Sons, 2016).
2. Ibid.
3. For simplicity, we use the term "features" to encapsulate what others might call product elements, characteristics, attributes, etc.
4. C. Whan Park, Bernard J. Jaworski, and Deborah J. MacInnis, "Strategic Brand Concept-Image Management," *Journal of Marketing* 50, no. 4 (1986): 135–45, doi:10.1177/002224298605000401.
5. Albert Bandura, *Self-Efficacy: The Exercise of Control* (New York: W. H. Freeman, 1997).
6. David Brinberg and Ronald Wood, "A Resource Exchange Theory Analysis of Consumer Behavior," *Journal of Consumer Research* 10, no. 3 (1983): 330–38, doi:10.1086/208972.
7. C. Whan Park, Deborah J. MacInnis, and Andreas B. Eisingerich, *Brand Admiration: Building a Business People Love* (Hoboken, NJ: John Wiley & Sons, 2016).
8. This example comes from ibid.
9. Peter F. Drucker, *The Practice of Management* (London: Routledge, 1954).
10. "Doorbell Camera Market Size, Share & Trends Report, 2025," accessed December 6, 2022, https://www.grandviewresearch.com/industry-analysis/doorbell-camera-market.

11. "Steve Jobs: 'There's Sanity Returning,'" Bloomberg, May 25, 1998, https://www.bloomberg.com/news/articles/1998-05-25/steve-jobs-theres-sanity-returning.
12. Carmine Gallo, "5 Reasons Why Steve Jobs's iPhone Keynote Is Still the Best Presentation of All Time," Inc.com, accessed December 6, 2022, https://www.inc.com/carmine-gallo/5-reasons-why-steve-jobs-iphone-keynote-is-still-the-best-presentation-of-all-ti.html.
13. Eric von Hippel, "The Dominant Role of Users in the Scientific Instrument Innovation Process," *Research Policy* 5, no. 3 (1976): 212–39, doi:10.1016/0048-7333(76)90028-7.
14. Eric von Hippel, *Free Innovation* (London: The MIT Press, 2017).
15. Marie Tae Mcdermott, "How Restaurants Have Weathered the Pandemic," *New York Times*, January 8, 2021, https://www.nytimes.com/2021/01/08/us/ca-covid-restaurants.html.
16. "How Restaurants Are Adapting and Transforming Their Businesses amid the Pandemic," Restaurant Business, April 29, 2021, https://www.restaurantbusinessonline.com/technology/how-restaurants-are-adapting-transforming-their-businesses-amid-pandemic.
17. Mutka Lad, "Looking Ahead: Key Marketing Trends Brands Should Focus On," accessed December 6, 2022, https://www-warc-com.libproxy1.usc.edu/content/article/event-reports/looking-ahead-key-marketing-trends-brands-should-focus-on/142329.
18. C. Whan Park, Deborah J. MacInnis, and Andreas B. Eisingerich, *Brand Admiration: Building a Business People Love* (Hoboken, NJ: John Wiley & Sons, 2016).
19. Natalie Mizik, "Assessing the Total Financial Performance Impact of Brand Equity with Limited Time-Series Data," *Journal of Marketing Research* 51, no. 6 (2014): 691–706, doi:10.1509/jmr.13.0431.
20. C. Whan Park, Andreas Eisingerich, and Jason Whan Park, "Attachment-Aversion (AA) Model of Customer–Brand Relationships," *Journal of Consumer Psychology* 23, no. 2 (2013): 229–48, doi:10.1016/j.jcps.2013.01.002.
21. Joo-Eon Jeon, "The Impact of Brand Concept on Brand Equity," *Asia Pacific Journal of Innovation and Entrepreneurship* 11, no. 2 (August 2017): 233–45, doi:10.1108/APJIE-08-2017-030.
22. "Customer Centricity Is No Longer Enough," WARC: The Feed, accessed December 6, 2022, https://www.warc.com/content/feed/customer-centricity-is-no-longer-enough/en-GB/5234.

23. C. K. Prahalad and Gary Hamel, "The Core Competence of the Corporation," *Harvard Business Review* (May–June 1990), https://hbr.org/1990/05/the-core-competence-of-the-corporation.

Play #2: Know Your Brand's *Benefits*

1. C. Whan Park, Deborah J. MacInnis, and Andreas B. Eisingerich, *Brand Admiration: Building a Business People Love* (Hoboken, NJ: John Wiley & Sons, 2016); Lucy Gill-Simmen et al., "Brand-Self Connections and Brand Prominence as Drivers of Employee Brand Attachment," *AMS Review* 8, no. 3–4 (2018): 128–46, doi:10.1007/s13162-018-0110-6.
2. Marty Swant, "The 2020 World's Most Valuable Brands," *Forbes*, accessed December 6, 2022, https://www.forbes.com/the-worlds-most-valuable-brands/.
3. "Morning Consult's Most Trusted Brands 2021," Morning Consult, November 10, 2022, https://morningconsult.com/most-trusted-brands-2021/.
4. Interbrand website homepage, accessed June 7, 2023, https://interbrand.com/.
5. Kevin Lane Keller, *Strategic Brand Management: Building, Measuring, and Managing Brand Equity* (Boston: Pearson, 2013).
6. Lucy Gill-Simmen, Deborah J. MacInnis, Andreas Eisingerich, and C. Whan Park, "Brand-Self Connections and Brand Prominence as Drivers of Employee Brand Attachment," *Academy of Marketing Science Review* 8, no. 3 (2018): 128–46, doi:10.1007/s13162-018-0110-6.
7. "Going from the Great Resignation to 'The Great Retention' and other 2022 priorities," *Fast Company*, December 31, 2021, https://www.fastcompany.com/90707830/going-from-the-great-resignation-to-the-great-retention-and-other-2022-priorities.
8. Michael Porter, "How Competitive Forces Shape Strategy," *Harvard Business Review* (March–April 1979), https://hbr.org/1979/03/how-competitive-forces-shape-strategy.
9. Tülin Erdem and Joffre Swait, "Brand Credibility, Brand Consideration, and Choice," *Journal of Consumer Research* 31, no. 1 (June 2004): 191–98, doi:10.1086/383434; Ronnie Ballantyne, Anne Warren, and Karinna Nobbs, "The Evolution of Brand Choice," *Journal of Brand Management* 13, no. 4 (2006): 339–52.
10. C. Whan Park et al., "Brand Attachment and Brand Attitude Strength: Conceptual and Empirical Differentiation of Two Critical Brand Equity Drivers," *Journal of Marketing* 74, no. 6 (2010): 1–17, doi:10.1509/jmkg.74.6.1.

11. Kevin Lane Keller, "Conceptualizing, Measuring, and Managing Customer-Based Brand Equity," *Journal of Marketing* 57, no. 1 (1993): 1–22, doi:10.1177/002224299305700101; Deborah Roedder John, Barbara Loken, Kyeongheui Kim, and Alokparna Basu Monga, "Brand Concept Maps: A Methodology for Identifying Brand Association Networks," *Journal of Marketing Research* 43, no. 4 (2006): 549–63, doi:10.1509/jmkr.43.4.549.
12. HaeEun Helen Chun, Kristin Diehl, and Deborah J. MacInnis, "Savoring an Upcoming Experience Affects Ongoing and Remembered Consumption Enjoyment," *Journal of Marketing* 81, no. 3 (2017): 96–110, doi:10.1509/jm.15.0267; Stuart J. Barnes, Jan Mattsson, and Flemming Sørensen, "Remembered Experiences and Revisit Intentions: A Longitudinal Study of Safari Park Visitors," *Tourism Management* 57 (2016): 286–94, doi:10.1016/j.tourman.2016.06.014.
13. Steve Hoeffler and Kevin Lane Keller, "The Marketing Advantages of Strong Brands," *Journal of Brand Management* 10, no. 6 (2003): 421–45, doi:10.1057/palgrave.bm.2540139.
14. Icek Ajzen, Marin Fishbein, Sophie Lohmann, and Dolores Albarracín, "The Influence of Attitudes on Behavior," in *The Handbook of Attitudes*, eds. Dolores Albarracín and Blaire T. Johnson (Mahwah, NJ: Lawrence Erlbaum Associates, 2005), 173–221; Russell H. Fazio and David R. Roskos-Ewoldsen, "Acting as We Feel: When and How Attitudes Guide Behavior," in *Persuasion: Psychological Insights and Perspectives*, eds. Timothy C. Brock and Melanie C. Green (Thousand Oaks, CA: Sage Publications: 2005): 41–62.
15. Joseph R. Priester, Dhananjay Nayakankuppam, Monique A. Fleming, and John Godek, "The A^2SC^2 Model: The Influence of Attitudes and Attitude Strength on Consideration and Choice," *Journal of Consumer Research* 30, no. 4 (2004): 574–87, doi:10.1086/380290.
16. Thomas J. Madden, Pamela Scholder Ellen, and Icek Ajzen, "A Comparison of the Theory of Planned Behavior and the Theory of Reasoned Action," *Personality and Social Psychology Bulletin* 18, no. 1 (1992): 3–9, doi:10.1177/0146167292181001.
17. "Two-Thirds of Brands Fall Short on Customer Experience," WARC: The Feed, accessed December 6, 2022, https://www.warc.com/content/feed/two-thirds-of-brands-fall-short-on-customer-experience/en-gb/5337.
18. Smitha Mundasad, "Victorian Keep-Fit Exercises and Gym Regimes Revealed," BBC News, September 27, 2014, https://www.bbc.com/news/health-28858090.

19. Hamza Shaban, "The Pandemic's Home-Workout Revolution May Be Here to Stay," *Washington Post*, January 8, 2021, https://www.washingtonpost.com/road-to-recovery/2021/01/07/home-fitness-boom/.
20. Sharon Terlep, "Peloton's Quarterly Loss Tops $1.2 Billion as Bike, Treadmill Sales Plunge," *Wall Street Journal*, August 25, 2022, https://www.wsj.com/articles/peloton-pton-q4-earnings-report-2022-11661390875.
21. MediaRadar, "Top Fitness Advertising Trends: DFD News," December 22, 2021, https://dfdnews.com/2021/12/22/top-fitness-advertising-trends/.
22. Lindsay Kolowich Cox, "The 18 Best Advertisements & Ad Campaigns of All Time," HubSpot, March 16, 2022, https://blog.hubspot.com/marketing/best-advertisements.

Play #3: Segment on Benefits

1. Wendell R. Smith, "Product Differentiation and Market Segmentation as Alternative Marketing Strategies," *Journal of Marketing* 21, no. 1 (1956): 3–8, doi:10.2307/1247695.
2. "51 Market Segmentation Examples," Intellspot.com, accessed December 6, 2022, http://www.intellspot.com/wp-content/uploads/2017/06/51-MARKET-SEGMENTATION-EXAMPLES.pdf.
3. Ben Schott, "Generation Z, You're Adorkable," Bloomberg, January 24, 2021, https://www.bloomberg.com/opinion/articles/2021-01-24/the-gen-z-brand-aesthetic-is-both-disruptive-and-adorkable.
4. "Cultural Insights Impact Measure™ (CIIM™)," Alliance for Inclusive and Multicultural Marketing, accessed December 6, 2022, https://www.anaaimm.net/resources/ciim.
5. Clayton M. Christensen, Scott Cook, and Taddy Hall, "Marketing Malpractice: The Cause and the Cure," *Harvard Business Review* (December 2005), https://hbr.org/2005/12/marketing-malpractice-the-cause-and-the-cure.
6. Michel Wedel and Wagner A. Kamakura, *Market Segmentation: Conceptual and Methodological Foundations* (New York: Springer Science+Business Media, 2000).
7. Ibid.
8. Matthew McGranaghan, Jura Liaukonyte, and Kenneth C. Wilbur, "How Viewer Tuning, Presence and Attention Respond to Ad Content and Predict Brand Search Lift," Marketing Science Institute Working Paper Series 2021, Report No. 21-132 (September 2021), https://www.msi.org/wp-content/uploads/2021/09/MSI_Report_21-132.pdf.

9. "What Is a Conjoint Analysis? Conjoint Types & When to Use Them," Qualtrics, April 6, 2022, https://www.qualtrics.com/au/experience-management/research/types-of-conjoint/.
10. Peloton, "What Is Peloton? It's Motivation That Moves You," The Output, Peloton, May 9, 2022, https://blog.onepeloton.com/peloton-motivation-that-moves-you/.
11. See, for example, Michael T. Brown and Lori R. Wicker, "Discriminant Analysis," in *Handbook of Applied Multivariate Statistics and Mathematical Modeling*, eds. Howard E. A. Tinsley and Steven D. Brown (San Diego: Academic Press: 2000): 209–235.
12. There are many excellent books on focus groups and how to conduct them. See, for example, David Morgan, *Basic and Advanced Focus Groups* (Los Angeles: Sage Publications, 2018); David Stewart and Prem N. Shamdasani, *Focus Groups: Theory and Practice* (Los Angeles: Sage Publications, 2014); and Richard A. Krueger and Mary Anne Casey, *Focus Groups: A Practical Guide for Applied Research* (Los Angeles: Sage Publications, 2014).

Play #4: Target and Position on Benefits

1. "Introducing LiMu Emu and Doug, the Dynamic Duo of the Insurance World Starring in New Liberty Mutual Ad Campaign," Liberty Mutual, accessed December 7, 2022, https://www.libertymutualgroup.com/about-lm/news/articles/introducing-limu-emu-and-doug-dynamic-duo-insurance-world-starring-new-liberty-mutual-ad-campaign.
2. "H. Dennis Beaver: Only Pay for What You Need," *Hanford Sentinel*, October 1, 2020, https://hanfordsentinel.com/opinion/columnists/h-dennis-beaver-only-pay-for-what-you-need/article_982ac962-98b6-5dfe-8ae8-e8f5236a04e2.html.
3. J. Clement, "Video Gaming Market Size Worldwide 2020–2025," Statista, April 17, 2023, https://www.statista.com/statistics/292056/video-game-market-value-worldwide/.
4. Chris Wilks, Bo Bothe, and Elizabeth Tindall, "Brand Analysis: Southwest Airlines," BrandExtract, accessed December 7, 2022, https://www.brandextract.com/Insights/Podcast-Episodes/Brand-Analysis-Southwest-Airlines/.
5. "The Untold Old Spice Story," Landor, accessed June 7, 2023, https://aef.com/wp-content/uploads/2016/10/landor_oldspice.pdf.

6. Advertising Education Foundation, "Pam Cooking Spray: Food Freedom," Case Study; see also PAM Creative Brief, Kimitatiana, accessed June 7, 2023, https://kimitatiana.files.wordpress.com/2017/07/pam-creative-brief.pdf.
7. "How to Write a Brand Positioning Statement," EquiBrand, May 31, 2022, https://equibrandconsulting.com/how-to-write-a-great-brand-positioning-statement.
8. Basha Coleman, "How to Write a Great Value Proposition [7 Top Examples + Template]," HubSpot, April 13, 2023, https://blog.hubspot.com/marketing/write-value-proposition; Geoffrey James, "4 Types of Basic Value Propositions," Inc.com, accessed December 7, 2022, https://www.inc.com/geoffrey-james/the-4-types-of-value-proposition.html.
9. "Unique Value Proposition," Institute for Strategy & Competitiveness, Harvard Business School, accessed December 7, 2022, https://www.isc.hbs.edu/strategy/creating-a-successful-strategy/Pages/unique-value-proposition.aspx.
10. Nicolas Liddell quoted in "Seven Steps to Effective Brand Positioning," WARC, August 8, 2016, https://www.warc.com/newsandopinion/news/seven-steps-to-brand-positioning/en-gb/37199.

Play #5: Pass the Credibility Stress Test

1. Michael E. Porter, *Competitive Advantage: Creating and Sustaining Superior Performance* (New York: Simon & Schuster, 1985).
2. Madison Iszler, "Rackspace Blames 'Security Incident' for Outage That's Taken out Email Services for Customers," *San Antonio Express-News*, December 6, 2022, https://www.expressnews.com/business/article/Rackspace-security-outage-17630736.php.
3. Theo Thimou, "Study: Walmart 34% Cheaper than Amazon, on Average," Clark.com, February 6, 2018, https://clark.com/personal-finance-credit/budgeting-saving/amazon-walmart-price-comparison/.
4. "IKEA Strengthens Commitments to Reduce Inequalities and Advance Human Rights," IKEA, September 28, 2022, https://about.ikea.com/en/newsroom/publications/ikea-sustainability-strategy--people--planet-positive.
5. Nora Eckert, "Ford's Latest Supply-Chain Problem: A Shortage of Blue Oval Badges," *Wall Street Journal*, September 23, 2022, https://www.wsj.com/articles/fords-latest-supply-chain-snarl-not-enough-blue-oval-badges-11663944141.

6. C. K. Prahalad and Gary Hamel, "The Core Competence of the Corporation," *Harvard Business Review* (May–June 1990), https://hbr.org/1990/05/the-core-competence-of-the-corporation.
7. Ibid.

Play #6: Pass the Defensibility Stress Test

1. See, for example, Steve Tadelis, *Game Theory: An Introduction* (Princeton, NJ: Princeton University Press, 2013).
2. Michael E. Porter, *Competitive Advantage: Creating and Sustaining Superior Performance* (New York: Free Press, 1985).
3. Leonard M. Fuld, *The New Competitor Intelligence: The Complete Resource for Finding, Analyzing, and Using Information About Your Competitors* (New York: John Wiley & Sons, 1995).
4. Michal Pecánek, "How to Conduct a Competitive Analysis (Template Included)," SEO Blog by Ahrefs, December 10, 2020, https://ahrefs.com/blog/competitor-analysis/.
5. "Brachistochrone Curve," Wikipedia, Wikimedia Foundation, November 24, 2022, https://en.wikipedia.org/wiki/Brachistochrone_curve.

Play #8: Activate on Benefits

1. If your brand is new to the market, you have an opportunity to select a brand name that best incorporates one or more key brand benefits. Descriptive brand names like "I Can't Believe It's Not Butter," "Almond Joy," and the citrus-scented dissolver "Citra Solv" are both memorable and useful vehicles for communicating the brands' essential benefits.
2. A tagline is a brief phrase that captures the essence of the message. Example taglines include Nike's "Just Do It," Airbnb's "Belong Anywhere," and Disneyland's "The Happiest Place on Earth."
3. For detailed information on each of these stages, see Wayne Hoyer, Deborah J. MacInnis, and Rik Pieter, *Consumer Behavior* (Boston: Cengage Learning, 2023).
4. Lori Wizdo, "The Ways and Means of B2B Buyer Journey Maps: We're Going Deep at Forrester's B2B Forum," Forrester, August 21, 2017, https://www.forrester.com/blogs/the-ways-and-means-of-b2b-buyer-journey-maps-were-going-deep-at-forresters-b2b-forum/

5. "Study: Half of B2B Buyers Make Up Their Minds Before Talking to Sales," PRWeb, June 5, 2018, https://www.prweb.com/releases/2018/06/prweb15537641.htm.
6. Heart of the Customer website homepage, accessed June 8, 2023, https://www.heartofthecustomer.com/.
7. For classic research on consideration set formation, see Allan D. Shocker, Moshe Ben-Akiva, Bruno Boccara, and Prakash Nedungadi, "Consideration Set Influences on Consumer Decision-Making and Choice: Issues, Models, and Suggestions," *Marketing Letters* 2, no. 3 (1991): 181–97; Amitav Chakravarti and Chris Janiszewski, "The Influence of Macro-Level Motives on Consideration Set Composition in Novel Purchase Situations," *Journal of Consumer Research* 30, no. 2 (2003): 244–58, doi:10.1086/376803. For classic research on persuasion and preference formation, see Richard E. Petty and John T. Cacioppo, "The Elaboration Likelihood Model of Persuasion," *Advances in Experimental Social Psychology* 19 (1986): 123–205, doi:10.1016/S0065-2601(08)60214-2; Deborah J. MacInnis and Bernard J. Jaworski, "Information Processing from Advertisements: Toward an Integrative Framework," *Journal of Marketing* 53, no. 4 (1989): 1–23, doi:10.2307/1251376. For classic research on persuasion and choice, see Icek Ajzen, Martin Fishbein, Sophie Lohmann, and Dolores Albarracín, "The Influence of Attitudes on Behavior," in *The Handbook of Attitudes*, edited by Dolores Albarracin and Blair T. Johnson (New York: Routledge, 2018), 197–255; Daniel Kahneman, *Thinking, Fast and Slow* (New York: Farrar, Straus and Giroux, 2013); Sheena Iyengar, *The Art of Choosing* (New York: Twelve, 2010). For research on the customer experience, see Bernd H. Schmitt, *Customer Experience Management: A Revolutionary Approach to Connecting with Your Customers* (New York: John Wiley & Sons, 2003); Christian Homburg, Danijel Jozić, and Christina Kuehnl, "Customer Experience Management: Toward Implementing an Evolving Marketing Concept," *Journal of the Academy of Marketing Science* 45, no. 3 (2017): 377–401; Leonard L. Berry, Lewis P. Carbone, and Stephan H. Haeckel, "Managing the Total Customer Experience," *MIT Sloan Management Review* 43, no. 3 (2002): 85–89. For classic research on postpurchase brand evaluations, see Richard L. Oliver, *Satisfaction: A Behavioral Perspective on the Consumer* (Routledge, 2014). For research on repurchase intentions, see Markus Blut, Carly M. Frennea, Vikas Mittal, and David L. Mothersbaugh, "How Procedural, Financial and Relational Switching Costs Affect Customer Satisfaction, Repurchase Intentions, and

Repurchase Behavior: A Meta-analysis," *International Journal of Research in Marketing* 32, no. 2 (2015): 226–29, doi:10.1016/j.ijresmar.2015.01.001. Wayne Hoyer, Deborah J. MacInnis, and Rik Pieter, *Consumer Behavior* (Boston: Cengage Learning, 2023) provides an overview of the research discussed in this endnote.

8. See also C. Whan Park, Deborah J. MacInnis, and Andreas B. Eisingerich, *Brand Admiration: Building a Business People Love* (Hoboken, NJ: John Wiley & Sons, 2016).
9. Wayne Hoyer, Deborah J. MacInnis, and Rik Pieters, *Consumer Behavior*, 8th ed. (Boston: Cengage Learning, 2023).
10. Robert B. Cialdini, *Influence, New and Expanded: The Psychology of Persuasion* (New York: Harper Business, 2021).
11. David Griner, "Liberty Mutual's Ads Are Going in Some Very Weird Directions, and It's Working," *Adweek*, July 24, 2019, https://www.adweek.com/agencies/liberty-mutuals-ads-are-going-in-some-very-weird-directions-and-its-working/.
12. Roy A. Young, Allen M. Weiss, and David W. Stewart, *Marketing Champions: Practical Strategies for Improving Marketing's Power, Influence and Business Impact* (Hoboken, NJ: John Wiley & Sons, 2006).

Play #9: Grow Your Brand

1. "Fewer Excuses for Not Doing a PC Backup," CNET, January 13, 2007, https://www.cnet.com/tech/services-and-software/fewer-excuses-for-not-doing-a-pc-backup/.
2. Jon Ying, "Meet the Team! (Part 1)," Dropbox, accessed December 6, 2022. https://blog.dropbox.com/topics/company/meet-the-team-part-1.
3. We distinguish brand extensions from line extensions. The latter use the existing brand name on a variant of the product. Examples include Skippy Peanut Butter Extra Chunky (extended from regular Skippy), Coke Zero (extended from regular Coke), and Baked Lays (extended from Classic Lays).
4. Vanitha Swaminathan, Richard J. Fox, and Srinivas K. Reddy, "The Impact of Brand Extension Introduction on Choice," *Journal of Marketing* 65, no. 4 (2001): 1–15, doi:10.1509/jmkg.65.4.1.18388; Susan M. Broniarczyk and Joseph W. Alba, "The Importance of the Brand in Brand Extension," *Journal of Marketing Research* 31, no. 2 (1994): 214–28, doi:10.2307/3152195.
5. Logan Fairbrother, "Gatorade Introduces New Smart Bottle and Gummies," Hypebeast, October 4, 2022, https://hypebeast.com/2022/10/gatorade-gx-smart-bottle-gummies-announcement-info.

6. Note that the Ivory soap brand and its brand extensions sit within P&G, which uses an independent branding architecture. Thus, a given brand in a "house of brands" like P&G can offer its own brand extensions.
7. Kevin Lane Keller, *Strategic Brand Management: Building, Measuring, and Managing Brand Equity* (Boston: Pearson Education, 2013).
8. C. Whan Park et al., "Brand Attachment and Brand Attitude Strength: Conceptual and Empirical Differentiation of Two Critical Brand Equity Drivers," *Journal of Marketing* 74, no. 6 (2010): 1–17, doi:10.1509/jmkg.74.6.1; C. Whan Park, Deborah J. MacInnis, and Andreas B. Eisingerich, *Brand Admiration: Building a Business People Love* (Hoboken, NJ: John Wiley & Sons, 2016).
9. C. Whan Park, Andreas Eisingerich, and Jason Whan Park, "Attachment-aversion (AA) Model of Customer–Brand Relationships," *Journal of Consumer Psychology* 23, no. 2 (2013): 229–48, doi:10.1016/j.jcps.2013.01.002.
10. C. Whan Park, Deborah J. MacInnis, and Andreas B. Eisingerich, *Brand Admiration: Building a Business People Love* (Hoboken, NJ: John Wiley & Sons, 2016); Andreas Eisingerich, Deborah J. MacInnis, and Martin Fleischman, "Moving Beyond Trust: Making Customers Trust, Love and Respect a Brand," *MIT Sloan Management Review*, December 13, 2021, https://sloanreview.mit.edu/article/moving-beyond-trust-making-customers-trust-love-and-respect-a-brand/.
11. C. Whan Park, Deborah J. MacInnis, and Andreas B. Eisingerich, *Brand Admiration: Building a Business People Love* (Hoboken, NJ: John Wiley & Sons, 2016).
12. See ibid. for an expansive perspective on brand admiration, including the science behind the concept, how employees within the organization can build brand admiration, the relationship between brand admiration and a company's mission statement, and how admired brands can be strengthened and leveraged, how admired brands add value to customers and companies, and how to build a brand admiration dashboard.

Final Words

1. Theodore Levitt, "Marketing Myopia," *Harvard Business Review* (May–June 2004), https://hbr.org/2004/07/marketing-myopia.

Appendices

1. "What Is Conjoint Analysis?," 1000minds, accessed December 7, 2022, https://www.1000minds.com/conjoint-analysis/what-is-conjoint-analysis.

2. Jerry Wind, Paul E. Green, Douglas Shifflet, and Marsha Scarbrough, "*Courtyard by Marriott*: Designing a Hotel Facility with Consumer-Based Marketing Models," *Interfaces* 19 (1989): 25–47.
3. Mark Compton, "Courtyard by Marriott Signals Brand Evolution to Reinvigorate Its North American Portfolio," Marriott International, December 8, 2021, https://news.marriott.com/news/2021/12/08/courtyard-by-marriott-signals-brand-evolution-to-reinvigorate-its-north-american-portfolio.
4. Eric Malcolm Rogers, *Diffusion of Innovations* (New York: Free Press, 1962).
5. Lucy Handley, "Physical Books Still Outsell e-Books—and Here's Why," CNBC, September 19, 2019, https://www.cnbc.com/2019/09/19/physical-books-still-outsell-e-books-and-heres-why.html.
6. The Marketer's Toolkit: Future Thinking 2022, WARC, accessed December 7, 2022, https://www.warc.com/reports/toolkit.
7. James Fox, "Marketing Trends in 2022: Consumer Insights and Data," WARC, accessed December 7, 2022, https://www-warc-com.libproxy1.usc.edu/content/article/warc-exclusive/marketing-trends-in-2022-consumer-insights-and-data/140420.
8. Brandon Purcell et al., "Predictions 2022: Customer Insights," Forrester, November 3, 2021, https://www.forrester.com/report/predictions-2022-customer-insights/RES176375.

ABOUT THE AUTHORS

Allen Weiss, PhD, is the founder and CEO of MarketingProfs, LLC, the largest B2B marketing training, consulting, and event company dedicated to helping large organizations, teams, and individuals execute marketing campaigns that drive actual results. MarketingProfs has over 600,000 subscribers, 440,000 Twitter followers, and 360,000 LinkedIn followers. He is also a consultant, conference speaker, and Emeritus Professor at the University of Southern California. Dr. Weiss has developed a rigorous process for benefit positioning in his consulting with global technology companies. His work can be seen in brands such as Intel, Texas Instruments, and Informix (an IBM company), as well as banks (Far East National Bank) and insurance companies (AIG).

Debbie MacInnis, PhD, is the Charles L. and Ramona I. Hilliard Professor of Business Administration and Emerita Professor of Marketing at the University of Southern California's Marshall School of Business. She is a globally recognized, multi-award-winning expert on evidence-based customer decision-making and brand strategies, emphasizing brand benefits, execution, and brand growth. Her awards include the University of Southern California Lifetime Achievement Award, a fellow of the American Marketing Association, and a fellow of the Association for Consumer Research. Debbie has consulted with many organizations such as Hallmark, Proctor & Gamble, the American Beverage Association, United Talent Agency, and major advertising companies. She also has been an expert witness for the Federal Trade Commission and other organizations.

SHIFT YOUR PERSPECTIVE

FOCUS FIRST ON THE BENEFITS YOUR CUSTOMERS SEEK WITH OUR HELP.

For additional resources and support to execute this playbook:

VISIT BRANDBENEFITSPLAYBOOK.COM